AFRAID TO ASK

JUDYLAINE FINE

Afraid to Ask

A BOOK ABOUT CANCER

Kids Can Press
Toronto

Kids Can Press gratefully acknowledges the assistance of the
Canada Council and the Ontario Arts Council in the production of this book.

Medical illustrations by Dorothy Irwin

Canadian Cataloguing in Publication Data

Fine, Judylaine.
  Afraid to ask: a book about cancer

Included index.
Bibliography: p
ISBN 0-919964-79-6 (bound).
ISBN 0-919964-56-7 (pbk.).

1. Cancer - Juvenile literature. I. Title.

RC263.F56 1984   j616.99'4   C84-098729-3

Typeset by Small Faces Typography Inc.
Printed in Canada by D.W. Friesen and Sons
Book and cover design by Michael Solomon
Kids Can Press, Toronto

For all the teenagers, mothers, and fathers
who have had the courage to share their pain . . .
and for Harold S. Fine who has always shown courage.

Table of Contents

Acknowledgements

I can't adequately express my gratitude to the people who helped make this book possible. By answering my thousands of questions and wading through my explanations with fine tooth combs, these dedicated people have shattered my impression that people in the health care professions are unwilling to share their time.

Dr. Richard Hasselback, senior medical oncologist at the Princess Margaret Hospital in Toronto, read and commented on the manuscript on three separate occasions. In a sense he is the godfather of *Afraid to Ask*.

The following people read and commented on the manuscript, and I am especially indebted to them: Alan Bernstein, Ph.D., molecular geneticist, Ontario Cancer Institute; Dr. Saul Levine, chief of psychiatry, Sunnybrook Hospital; Anthony Miller, Ph.D., director, epidemiology unit, National Cancer Institute of Canada; Cheryl Moyer, national assistant director of public education, Canadian Cancer Society; David Nostbakken, Ph.D., national director of public education, Canadian Cancer Society; Dr. Harry Schachter, head, research division, department of biochemistry, Hospital for Sick Children.

I am also grateful to the following people who granted me interviews: Bill Adair, national director of service to patients, Canadian Cancer Society; David Adams, M.S.W., director of social work services, McMaster University Medical Centre; Margaret Arnold, Cansurmount Convener, Metropolitan Toronto, Canadian Cancer Society; Dr. Michael Baker, chief of oncology, Toronto General Hospital; Marilyn Deachman, psychosocial liaison nurse, Princess Margaret Hospital; Dr. Barry DeVebber, director of hematology oncology, Victoria Hospital, London, Ontario; Dr. Hans Dosch, associate professor of paediatrics, division of immunology and rheumatology, department of paediatrics, Hospital for Sick Children; Gerrit DeBoer, Ph.D., head, department of biostatistics, Ontario Cancer Institute; Stephen Fleming, Ph.D., associate professor of psychology, York University; Dr. Erwin Gelfand, chief, division of immunology and rheumatology, department of paediatrics, Hospital for Sick Children; Mark Greenberg, senior oncologist, division of hematology oncology, department of paediatrics, Hospital for Sick Children; Zsolt Harsanyi, Ph.D., executive director, Porton International Ltd., New York; Joseph Hoffman, program director, Project D.A.R.E.; Gabriel Lam, Ph.D., research biophysicist, Medical Biophysics Unit, B.C. Cancer Research Centre; Gordon Lang, bereavement counsellor, Victoria Hospital, London, Ontario; Dr. Dorothy Ley, executive director, The Palliative Care Foundation of Canada; The Reverend Pam McGee, director of chaplaincy services, The Wellesley and Princess Margaret Hospitals; Marilyn MacKenzie, former head nurse, department of hematology oncology, Hospital for Sick Children; Dr. Ed Pakes, senior psychiatrist, Hospital for Sick Children; Dr. Ralph Pohlman, consulting psychiatrist, Sunnybrook Hospital; Peter Scholefield, Ph.D., executive director, National Cancer Institute of Canada; Dr. Michel Silberfeld, staff psychiatrist, Princess Margaret Hospital; Mary Vachon, Ph.D., research scientist, Clark Institute of Psychiatry.

I would also like to thank the Canadian Cancer Society for generously providing me with material on many specific types of cancer.

Introduction

Two decades ago, when I was a teenager, the word "cancer" was rarely spoken. The disease was prevalent, but not discussed. In most families, adults avoided answering any questions we might have had about cancer. And, in fact, most of us never dared to ask.

Things have changed. Today, many adults realize that teenagers want to know the truth about cancer. The trouble is that while we want to satisfy your needs, knowing what to say, and how best to say it, is very difficult. In some instances, our own knowledge is lacking. In other instances, there are simply no answers. All of us — even scientists — are asking the same questions as you.

While scientists have learned what cancer is, for example, they still don't know many of the details that occur when a normal cell changes into a cancer cell. While they are aware of some of the factors that can increase a person's risk of developing cancer, they don't know exactly why one person gets the disease while another person does not.

Doctors know that almost half of the people who get cancer will beat it. But they don't know for sure who will be in which half. This means they don't know for certain what will happen to the person you are worried about.

In an attempt to protect you from emotional pain, many adults leave facts unsaid. I have written this book because I believe very strongly that teenagers are entitled to as much information about cancer as they need. *Afraid to Ask* tries to answer as many questions as possible, as directly as possible.

The first chapter explains what cancer is. If you are fascinated by scientific details, you will find them here. When I first began to do the research for this book, the science of cancer wasn't my main interest. Then I met Dr. Harry Schachter, a biochemist at the Hospital for Sick Children in Toronto, and I became intrigued. I wouldn't be surprised if the same thing happens to you.

But if understanding what cancer really is doesn't interest you as much as knowing who gets the disease, or how doctors treat it, go right to the chapter you feel a need to understand. If knowing about a particular type of cancer is what you are after, turn to the last section of the book. I have organized *Afraid to Ask* in such a way that it is not essential to start at page one.

As for the questions for which there are still no answers, researchers are pressing ahead. Each day, it seems, more and more clues that could eventually lead to a cure for cancer are emerging. Scientists have never been more hopeful than they are today.

In the meantime, until these remaining mysteries can be solved, you will know at least that other people are asking too. Ninety thousand Canadians are diagnosed with cancer every year. You are not alone in what you are going through.

PART I
Afraid to Ask

CHAPTER ONE

What is Cancer?

"**M**Y MOM has had cancer. If I could only wrap my brain around what cancer is, I think somehow I'd be able to handle it better."

Jenny was 16 when I met her. She had already been through a two-year battle with breast cancer — her mother's. Things were looking fairly hopeful by the time I talked to her. But those two years had been awful. First there had been surgery. Then gruelling treatments with radiation and chemicals — chemotherapy they call it — that left Jenny wondering how a treatment with such terrible side effects could possibly *cure* someone of a disease.

Jenny had read everything about cancer she could get her hands on: pamphlets she found in the visitors' lounge at Toronto's Princess Margaret Hospital for cancer treatment; newspaper clippings; magazine articles. And yet, she still sensed that she didn't have a handle on what was going on.

"I know that every year almost 90,000 Canadians get cancer," she told me. "I mean, I've read that. I've read that and a bunch of other figures a thousand times. But how does cancer start? Why can't doctors always cure it? What does it look like? How come it starts in one place and ends up in another? I must have asked two dozen people these questions — doctors, teachers — but no one has ever given me answers that really make sense."

A lot of things about cancer hadn't made much sense to me either. But I had been lucky. When I had put out the word that

I was working on this book, many professionals agreed to talk to me. Everyone was excited that a book on cancer was being written for teenagers.

The week before I met Jenny, my understanding of cancer had suddenly increased by leaps and bounds. Someone had suggested I speak to Dr. Harry Schachter, a cancer researcher at Toronto's Hospital for Sick Children.

Dr. Schachter's down-to-earth explanations boomed across the room. "The trouble is, we don't really understand the *basics* of cancer. No one even knows why cancer starts.

"Why does a normal cell that's doing what it's supposed to do *stop* doing what it's supposed to be doing and become cancerous? What makes a cancer cell — unlike a normal cell — able to break off from the organ where it belongs?"

Dr. Schachter paused a moment for emphasis. "Did you know that a cancerous liver cell can move from the liver to set up shop in another organ — say the lung — where it grows into a second cancer tumour? Any *normal* liver cell would be dead in no time if it somehow got detached from its liver and found its way to a lung. The body doesn't let normal liver cells live in lungs. It doesn't let them live anywhere, except in livers!

"The thing is, until we figure out the answers to all these questions, the cure for cancer will remain out of reach. And no one can say for sure when researchers will find these answers."

There are many things about cancer that scientists do know. They know what cancer looks like, for example. Often they know how to treat it successfully — if it has been detected at an early stage. The trouble is, by the time a lot of cancers are discovered, they have had time to grow into hard, gritty tumours, at least the size of a pea. Frequently, the first or primary tumour has "shed" some of its cells which have travelled to other parts of the body and grown into secondary tumours. Then there is more than one tumour to treat.

Some types of cancer grow in clusters that look, to the naked eye, like cauliflowers. Other kinds look more like the flesh of sliced fish. Still others, breast cancer for example, have fingers that radiate haphazardly like crab grass into nearby tissue. In fact, the word "cancer" means crab, the animal with claws that radiate from the main part of its body.

But if you were to take a paper thin slice of a cancer tumour and slap it between two pieces of glass under a microscope, what you'd see might surprise you. Many researchers have used the word majestic to describe the look of magnified cancer cells. One man, a doctor called John MacDonald, died of lung cancer not long after he wrote *When Cancer Strikes*. He described cancer cells as seen under a microscope as "a forest fire . . . a flock of birds frightened from their destined path . . . scattered in disarray." I think they look like the swirls of a multicoloured marble cake all ready to be baked.

While there are different descriptions of how cancer cells look, no one disagrees about how they perform. Cancer cells no longer do the job they are supposed to be doing. What's worse, they no longer act in the orderly way that cells in our bodies normally act. Instead, cancer cells divide like crazy, without rhyme or reason, without any regard for the rest of the body's needs. They may be liver cells in a liver that doesn't need any new cells and yet they continue to reproduce. They may be liver cells that have detached themselves from their liver and are living in a lung, or in a brain, or anywhere. As Dr. Schachter explained, a normal liver cell that had somehow broken off from its liver would never be allowed by the body to set up shop in another organ. Somehow, cancer cells can.

But the only way to grasp the mystery of cancer is to begin with the basics. Until you have an understanding of how cells are supposed to work, it's impossible to really understand what happens when things go wrong.

How Cancer Cells Work

To begin with, cancer is not a single disease. There are more than 100 different kinds of cancer. Scientists have been able to show that different things, certain chemicals, radiation, and some viruses, can cause cancer. Basically, cancer is a disturbance in cell physiology — the mechanics of how a cell works.

How a cell works is an extremely complicated matter. Cells are not, for example, like cars. When your car isn't running properly, you take it to a mechanic. He knows where every bolt goes, what every piston does, and what makes the car's engine go. It's relatively easy to fix something when you understand its mechanics.

Unfortunately, how normal cells work is not yet understood, not by a long shot! In the past 10 years, scientists have unravelled a great number of mysteries. But many basic questions still remain unanswered.

Scientists don't understand, for example, how a cell knows what its particular job is. They don't understand how some of the cells in the liver know that their job is to produce proteins that can purify blood. Or how these same liver cells also know when it's time to reproduce by dividing into two new liver cells to replace ones that have gotten old and died. Scientists also have very little idea how these cells know that it's time to *stop* reproducing when there are just the right number of new liver cells.

Until these riddles are solved, scientists won't be able to explain why cancer cells stop following the rules that govern all normal cells.

But let's go all the way back to the beginning. Imagine that millions of years ago, there was a great big pot of stew — the universe. Everything was rolling around in the stew, bubbling away, and then . . . the first basic development occurred: a membrane was born.

The membrane was an amazing evolutionary leap. Without it, there was nothing to protect all molecules from the destructive aspects of the environment. Think of this membrane as a little plastic bag. In it, molecules could develop without being attacked by the environment outside.

Over millions of years, the molecules in that primitive little bag did develop, and eventually, the cell as we know it today evolved. So now, we have a cell surrounded by a membrane. There are trillions of cells in one human body.

But if you were to look at one of these cells with a microscope, you'd see that there are even smaller bags within it which are also surrounded by protective membranes. One

Cell Division (Mitosis)

Normal Cell Division

Abnormal Cell Division
(Often found in cancer)

Centrioles
(2 pairs) Nucleus

Centrioles
(3 pairs) Nucleus

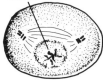

Normal – Division begins:
one pair of centrioles
duplicates.
Abnormal – Division begins:
one pair of centrioles
becomes 3 pairs.

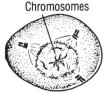

Chromosomes

Chromosomes

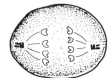

Normal & Abnormal
Centrioles move apart.
Chromosomes appear.

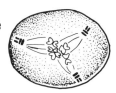

Normal – Chromosomes line
up in centre plane.
Abnormal – Chromosomes
overlap in centre.

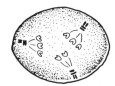

Normal & Abnormal
Chromosomes pull apart
and separate.

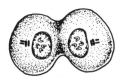

Normal & Abnormal
Cell begins to divide.
Nucleus re-appears.

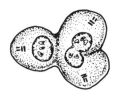

Normal – Cell divides into
two equal cells.
Abnormal – Cell divides into
3 unequal cells.

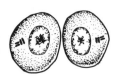

of these little bags, the most important one of all, is called the nucleus.

The nucleus of the cell contains the cell's genes which determine such things as the colour of our hair and eyes, our height, and thousands of other things like that. Scientists say that the nucleus of a cell "handles its genetics."

When you start off in life, your body doesn't have trillions of cells. It has only one cell, the result of your mother's egg uniting with your father's sperm. It's an amazing combination; in this first cell's nucleus are 46 strands called chromosomes. Twenty-three are from your mom, and 23 are from your dad.

Within each chromosome is a long line of genes which is made up of DNA, deoxyribonucleic acid.

Amazing as it seems, if you could count all the genes sitting along the chromosomes in the nucleus of one of your cells, you'd get something like 100,000 genes. The incredible thing is, the nucleus of *every* cell in your body contains the exact same 100,000 genes.

The second you are conceived, the egg and the sperm unite to make the first cell of the embryo. That's the blueprint — the special set of genes that makes up you. Then, something happens. First, the 46 chromosomes double and then the nucleus of this cell divides, or splits, into two. Then the rest of the cell divides, and you end up with two cells, both exactly the same as the first cell *and* each other. Both "daughter cells," as scientists call the two cells that form when one cell splits, have 46 chromosomes and the same 100,000 genes. It's as if the first cell, the blueprint, went to a photocopy machine and made a couple of copies of itself. As long as the machine is working properly, those two copies will be exactly the same as the original.

Then, these two cells divide and become four cells. The four cells divide and become eight cells, and then 16 cells, and pretty soon — in nine months to be exact — you've got trillions of cells that, altogether, make up a person.

Small wonder you'd want to put a membrane around something as important as the cell's nucleus to protect its contents from all the potentially dangerous things in the environment!

I thought about Dr. Schachter's explanation for a few weeks, but there was something about it that I didn't quite follow. I understood that one cell became two cells and that two cells became four cells. And I could see that all these cells contained the same 100,000 genes. But I couldn't understand how any one cell could possibly know that it had to go and become a liver cell, or a blood cell, or a brain cell.

At the very beginning, when there have been, say, only three cell divisions, there will be only eight cells, all exactly the same. They will all have the same 100,000 genes, some for hair colour, others for eye colour, some to produce blood, others to purify blood, and some to just keep house. (Cells like to keep themselves neat.) But at this point, these eight cells don't produce blood, or purify blood. All they do is divide.

But if the result of all this cell division is going to be a baby rather than just a blob of dividing cells, then very soon these cells have to differentiate — become *different types* of cells — brain cells, liver cells, blood cells, kidney cells. How does this happen?

How does a cell know that it's supposed to become a particular kind of cell with a specific job? How do some cells figure out that their job is to become blood cells? And never mind becoming just any blood cells, they have to know to become *particular kinds* of blood cells.

After all, some blood cells — white blood cells — have the job of fighting off infection. Other blood cells — red blood cells — carry oxygen around the body. Still other blood cells — blood stem cells — have the job of reproduction; they divide to produce new daughter blood cells as older blood cells wear out and die. These daughter blood stem cells are immature to begin with. Soon they grow into mature blood cells that perform the essential jobs taken care of by the blood in our bodies.

Another example: How do some of the first cells figure out that they have to become mature liver cells that can purify blood? Even more astounding is that mature liver cells not only know how to purify blood, they also know how to reproduce daughter liver cells. The liver is one organ that doesn't have "stem" cells whose only job is to reproduce daughter cells when additional cells are needed to replace old cells that have died. In the case of the liver, mature cells somehow know that sometimes their job is to purify blood and other times their job is to reproduce.

The first few cells of an embryo don't know all these things. But by the time a baby is born, all the cells have figured out that they have a very special job, or jobs, to do.

If that's going to happen, then in any particular cell, some of the 100,000 genes will have to work, and others will have to *not work*. How could a liver cell purify blood if its gene for hair production is working? It couldn't. A liver cell can only purify blood if its blood-purifying genes *and no other genes* (other than housekeeping genes) are in operation. What makes the whole matter even more complicated is that when it's time for the liver cell to stop purifying blood and start dividing, the gene for blood purification must stop working. And the gene for reproduction – the growth gene – must start.

Imagine a cell knowing how to do all of that!

The more I thought about it, the more impossible it all seemed. As it turned out, however, it wasn't so surprising that all this information about genes and their jobs was confusing. What seemed to me to be impossible to comprehend happens to be the tremendously complex process that baffles cancer researchers all over the world. They have been trying to understand exactly how genes work, for years.

Exactly what makes some genes in a cell work and other genes not work is one of the basic questions that scientists have spent millions of dollars trying to answer. It is the main obstacle that keeps people from being able to totally understand the mystery of cancer.

How Genes Work

The remarkable question of why some genes in one cell work and other genes in the same cell do not work has to do with a process which scientists call "differentiation." It means that a cell, with 100,000 or so genes somehow knows that it has one, or sometimes a few, specific jobs to perform. The job might require the activation of only a few of the cell's 100,000 genes — or sometimes, as is the case with a liver cell — different genes at different times. And it is just as important that all the other genes remain passive, or inactive.

For example, only a few out of all the 100,000 genes in a liver cell might be concerned with producing proteins that can purify blood. When that liver cell is going to purify some blood, then the rest of the genes had better do nothing. Imagine the chaos if a gene for eye colour in a liver cell suddenly started producing proteins for blue eyes, instead of purifying blood.

Only one of all the genes in a liver cell — the growth gene — signals that liver cell that it's time to divide into two new liver cells. And it is essential that the growth gene remain inactive when the liver does not happen to need any new cells.

A cell must stick to doing one job at any one time. And so, only one gene (or sometimes a group of a few genes) must be turned on.

In the case of blood cells, this process is a bit less complicated. A particular blood cell, unlike a liver cell, has only one job to worry about. Red blood cells carry oxygen and blood stem cells make daughter blood cells. Therefore, a blood cell only has to worry about turning one gene on or off. When the cell is supposed to perform its one job, the appropriate gene must turn on. When the cell is not supposed to perform its job, that same gene must turn off.

Imagine for a moment, what would happen if the growth gene in a blood stem cell started working at the wrong time, when the blood didn't need any new blood cells. You'd get more and more and more blood stem cells. Eventually, they'd take over the entire blood stream.

A similar problem would occur if the growth gene in a liver cell started working at the wrong time. You'd get more and more and more liver cells. Your liver would keep getting bigger and bigger.

Turn-ons and Turn-offs

How does a gene know when it's time for it to start working or stop working? Scientists believe that mechanisms called "turn-ons" and "turn-offs" tell genes when to start work-ing and when to stop.

Although you'd think that most of the space on the 46 chromosomes is taken up by all the genes, it's not so. Even more space is taken up by turn-ons and turn-offs. Unfor-tunately, scientists don't understand them very well. All they know is that turn-ons and turn-offs tell genes when they should start working, and when they should stop.

Take a liver cell as an example. When the body needs some blood purified, the environment tells the cell. Then a turn-on will signal the blood-purifying gene nearby: "Hey, the blood around here needs purifying. Make a protein that will get this cell of ours to purify some blood."

When some liver cells have died, perhaps of old age, the liver will get a bit too small. Again, the liver cell knows this because it is sensitive to its environment. In this case, another turn-on will say to the cell's growth gene: "I see that this liver of ours is getting a little puny. Seems we could use a few more cells." And it will signal the cell to divide into two new liver cells.

That's what the cell's turn-ons do.

The turn-offs perform jobs that are, in some ways, even more incredible. For one thing, they make sure that all the other genes in the liver cell — the ones for hair colour, eye colour, height, all of which are there, don't ever turn on. After all, you wouldn't want a hair gene in a liver cell making hair!

As well, once enough blood is purified, a turn-off will tell the blood-purifying gene to turn off, until more blood purifi-cation becomes necessary.

After some liver cells have divided and the liver is back to the size it's supposed to be, the appropriate turn-off does one of the most important jobs of all. It says "STOP!" to the growth gene. "No more new liver cells right now, growth gene, thank you very much." If it didn't, our livers would get too big.

One of the things that happens when you have liver cancer is your liver gets too big. Either the turn-off doesn't tell the growth gene to stop, or the growth gene no longer listens; scientists are not sure which it is. A growth gene gets turned on and for some reason, it never gets turned off again. You get more and more and more liver cells.

To make matters worse, these liver cells aren't differentiated properly anymore. They no longer know that in addition to dividing, they are also supposed to perform another special job — purifying blood. Just like the first cells that existed when the egg and sperm had only divided a few times, these cancerous cells can't do much more than divide. They forget that they are supposed to have evolved to the point where they not only know how to divide, but how to do other things as well. That's another important aspect of cancer to understand: genes that are supposed to get turned on don't get turned on. Cells stop being differentiated. They can't perform specific jobs.

Again, blood cells are a bit different. Normally, when the blood needs more cells, a turn-on in a blood stem cell will signal the growth gene to begin the division process. Two daughter blood stem cells will be produced. But soon, these daughter cells mature. They differentiate into mature blood cells that can perform a particular job. When there doesn't happen to be a need for more blood cells, the growth gene in the blood stem cell will turn off.

When a growth gene in a blood stem cell doesn't turn off, more and more blood stem cells will be produced. That's one of the things that happens when a person has leukemia, a cancer of the blood. But what makes this situation so bad is that the daughter cells produced by a cancerous blood stem cell remain immature. They never differentiate to the point of being capable of doing a specific job. Immature white blood cells, for example, are not able to guard the body against infection.

Cancerous blood stem cells, like cancerous liver cells, are only good at one thing — dividing. And while they divide — far more quickly, by the way, than normal cells — they compete with the rest of the body for vitamins, minerals, and other nutrients.

Cancer cells also happen to be more aggressive than normal

cells and for this reason, they monopolize these nutrients, weakening the cancer patient even further.

Eventually, tumours can get so big that they actually press on nearby organs, nerves, or bones. That's one of the reasons why cancer is sometimes so painful. A tumour can take over an organ completely and stop it from functioning at all. If that organ happens to be one which a person can't live without, like the liver, the person will die.

But the biggest problem is that undetected cancer tumours, and those that do not respond to treatment, can actually spread to other parts of the body. "Metastasize" is the word that doctors use. It means that cancer cells can start off in one place and end up in another.

A cancerous liver cell, for example, can move to a lung and "seed" itself. It can start growing into a cancerous liver tumour right in that lung.

Eventually, the cells from that cancerous liver might spread to a third organ and start growing a third tumour, and then to a fourth organ, and so on. Not only will the original, or primary, tumour interfere with the function of the first organ, it will also hinder the function of the organs to which it has spread.

In fact, that's the most dramatic aspect of cancer, and what makes it so hard to treat. A cancer tumour is not as difficult to deal with if it is discovered and destroyed before *even one* of its cells has had a chance to break off from the first tumour and spread.

It's important to understand that there is nothing about cancer cells that is actually *poisonous*, not in the sense that a copperhead snake's venom is so deadly. Many people have the idea that cancer is like something from outer space that takes over a person's body. It's not.

Cancer develops from cells that were once normal. Its deadliness comes from the fact that it spreads, and as it does, it interferes with so many of the body's normal functions that eventually, nothing works at all.

Why Do Cells Become Cancerous?

It was Dr. Schachter's explanation that helped me understand what happens when someone gets cancer. Cells, for some reason we don't completely understand, lose their ability to know how to behave properly as part of a finely balanced machine.

Why does this happen? Scientists believe it happens because, somehow, the cell's growth gene gets changed. The word they use is "mutate." Once a growth gene becomes mutated, it seems that it can cause other mechanisms in the cell to stop working properly as well, and the whole cell goes haywire. Nobody knows for sure, but many scientists think that a cancer tumour may actually start from one single cell that contains a mutated growth gene that has begun signalling itself to divide out of control.

Probably all the genes in all of our cells have the *potential* — the ability — to change or mutate and, in fact, sometimes do.

Gene mutations are serious, but not always related to cancer. A mutation may not do any harm at all to the person in whose body it has occurred. It might, however, show up a generation or two down the road. This is the type of genetic mutation you might have read about in connection with a chemical or drug.

Over the past few years, cancer researchers have been discovering specific genes which are related to cancer. If one of these genes becomes mutated, its cell can change into a cancer cell. So far, scientists have found 22 such genes. These genes are called "proto oncogenes," or potential cancer genes. If and when a proto oncogene does mutate, the "proto" gets dropped and the changed gene is called an "oncogene."

The name oncogene makes sense when you know that "onco" means tumour, or mass. "Proto" is short for prototype, which means "the type that occurs before." Proto oncogene is the gene that exists before a cancer gene occurs.

Research on oncogenes started in the U.S. about a decade ago. A group of scientists looked at a cancer cell, realized that it contained a mutated gene which had caused it to become cancerous, and named it an oncogene. Eventually, they realized that this oncogene had once been a perfectly normal growth gene which had somehow mutated. That's why normal growth genes — genes that have the potential to cause cancer — were called proto oncogenes.

The search for something in cancer cells that could explain why they had become abnormal had taken a long time. In fact, it hadn't been possible for scientists to even begin to study genes until some amazing tiny, biochemical tools were invented. These tools could actually slice a piece of DNA into its thousands of genes so that each miniscule piece of DNA could be examined. Discovering that cancerous cells have something in common — that they contain oncogenes — was considered to be a major breakthrough in cancer research.

Proto oncogenes that have the potential to cause cancer are in the cells of every person. It's scary to think of them, like tiny time-bombs ticking silently away. But most of the time, they don't mutate. They remain *growth* genes and play a perfectly normal and important role, just like all the other genes in every cell. They control cell reproduction, turning on *if and when* the cell is supposed to divide, otherwise remaining turned off.

How a Gene Becomes an Oncogene

The role of these 22 growth genes — proto oncogenes — is to regulate cell division. Many scientists explain the theory like this: when an organ requires more cells, a turn-on signals the cell's growth gene to become active. The growth gene tells the cell to divide. When a turn-off signals the growth gene to become inactive, the cell does not divide. As long as everything in the cell is functioning normally, a growth gene will only become active when there is a need for cell division. When there is no need, the growth gene will stay turned off, the cell will not divide, and there will be no problem.

But sometimes — a one-in-a-million chance — a growth gene will mutate into an oncogene. Just a tiny change, or more likely a couple of tiny changes, in the many parts of a growth gene, and it becomes an oncogene capable of changing its cell into a cancer cell.

Researchers believe that gene mutations occur most often while a cell is in the middle of dividing. Genes are most vulnerable to mutation while they are doubling.

Suppose you are in the middle of planting a new row of corn seeds in your garden right beside the row of corn seeds you planted yesterday. Let's say that the new row is the DNA of a new daughter cell, and that the seeds in this row are all its genes.

Let's also say that somehow, while you are planting this new row of corn seeds which is supposed to be exactly the same as the old row, you look away for a second, and someone sticks an Indian corn seed in the new row.

This would be as if a dividing cell produced a gene for its daughter cell that wasn't quite the same as it was in the old cell: an Indian corn seed where a regular corn seed ought to be.

That's what happens when a gene mutates. Somehow, a cell that's in the middle of dividing, sticks in a little piece of new cell that isn't right — a changed, or mutated gene. Once the cell division is complete, that tiny bit of damage in the new cell will be permanent. It will come up in all future cell divisions.

If the mutation has happened to a proto oncogene rather than any other gene, changing it into an oncogene, the new cell could become a cancer cell and cause a cancerous tumour to grow. Scientists believe that more than one mutation is necessary for this to happen, and the mutations could be spaced over many years.

For example: say a couple of mutations occur and a growth gene in a liver cell mutates into an oncogene. The oncogene couldn't care less whether or not the liver happens to need any more cells at that particular moment. It will turn on and signal the cell — now a cancer cell — to divide regardless. It will also cause the rest of the cell to go haywire.

Soon there will be two cancer cells, four cancer cells, then eight. Eventually, cancer cells will take over the entire liver. But exactly how all this begins is the big and still unanswered question.

So far, there are only theories about how, and why, a growth gene might mutate.

How and Why Genes Mutate

Dr. Alan Bernstein, who is working on several projects involving oncogenes for the Ontario Cancer Institute, explained some of the theories of gene mutations.

"Scientists believe that in some instances, a growth gene, a proto oncogene, moves from the chromosome where it's supposed to be to another chromosome where it's not supposed to be. In a case like this, the mutation is in the location of the gene, rather than in the gene itself. If a proto oncogene is suddenly in the wrong place, so this theory goes, a nearby turn-on might get confused — 'Who is this gene anyway, and what's it doing here?' — and tell it to turn on by mistake. The gene will then start signalling its cell to divide, whether new cells are needed or not. What's more, once it gets going, this oncogene never turns off.

"In other cases, scientists believe that a proto oncogene doesn't move to another chromosome, but somehow becomes mutated right where it is. Once the gene is changed, it no longer responds properly to turn-ons and turn-offs. It just turns on and stays on.

"In either case, you can imagine what will happen. The oncogene will start signalling the cell to divide, and divide, and divide."

What could cause a growth gene to move to another chromosome and become an oncogene? Or, what could cause a growth gene that hasn't moved to mutate into an oncogene? What is it that gets a gene that's working normally to go on the rampage?

Scientists have identified a number of things — certain chemicals, X-rays, and even a couple of viruses — which can cause human genes to mutate.

"We know that certain chemicals can cause growth genes to move or mutate," says Dr. Bernstein. "A number of the chemicals in cigarette smoke, for example, can definitely cause a growth gene to become an oncogene." Scientists have identified about 30 other chemicals that can cause human genes to mutate.

"In other instances," says Dr. Bernstein, "we researchers feel that the culprit is too much radiation." In laboratories, scientists have been able to demonstrate that high levels of radiation, or low levels whose effects have built up over time, can sometimes cause a gene to either move or mutate, or both.

In certain cases, scientists feel that a virus is to blame, although only two viruses have been found that can mutate human genes and they are very rare.

"And," says Dr. Bernstein, "mutations may sometimes just happen. Maybe there's a reason and maybe it has to do with heredity; we really don't know.

"When we have been able to demonstrate that a certain substance can cause a growth gene to mutate into a cancer-causing oncogene, we call the substance a 'carcinogen'. The word means cancer-causing."

Why Cells Follow Rules

Our bodies have several amazing systems that try to ensure that things don't go wrong. The first system that comes into play repairs genes that somehow get slightly damaged while they are doubling.

A second system, called the immune system, is manned by white blood cells and protects us from alien, nasty cells and microbes, like bacteria, that sometimes invade our bodies from outside. Many scientists believe that this system may also be able to destroy cells which have escaped the first fail-safe system and have become mutated into cancer cells.

As well, there is even a third system to ensure that cells of one type stay put in the organ where they belong. Normal liver cells can't just metastasize, or break off from the liver, travel to a lung, and live there. Cancer cells, however, can metastasize. When they grow into secondary tumours and take over a number of vital organs, they become deadly.

The first system, the one for repairing genes, works when any sort of gene gets damaged. The damage may be caused by a carcinogen or, it may just happen spontaneously. In any case, say the damage has occured to a gene in a cell that is right in the middle of dividing.

Cells are very clever about repairing this sort of damage. If a carcinogen does happen to cause a mutation to a gene while it is doubling, the cell can — and usually does — correct this damage.

Each cell actually has a repair shop which watches out for genetic errors. As the thousands of "bases," or tiny parts, of a new gene are being formed, this repair shop will usually notice if even one of those bases is incorrect. It also has the ability to correct a mistake *before* the dividing process is finished. When the repair shop sees a bit of new genetic material that contains an error — an Indian corn seed where a regular corn seed ought to be — it destroys this error and replaces it with the right stuff.

In fact, this repair process is going on all the time. Low levels of radiation are always coming down from the sky and doing damage to genes as they double. Chemicals are frequently interfering with our lives. But the repair shop is also always on the alert, working away. It usually corrects the damage before the cell division is complete, before the damage becomes permanent, leading to more defective cells and possibly to a cancerous tumour.

But let's say that somehow — and we'll get to some of the reasons in the next chapter — a gene in a dividing cell suffers some damage which the repair shop doesn't manage to catch on time.

What if the repair shop misses an error, and the cell completes its division? The new cell will contain a damaged gene — perhaps a damaged *growth* gene, an oncogene. What then? Can one of the other systems recognize that this cell is potentially dangerous? Is there a system that can kill this abnormal cell — this cancer cell — in self-defence? Is there a back-up mechanism if the first repair mechanism fails?

Some scientists believe the answer is yes. The body can get rid of at least a certain number of cancer cells that the genetic repair shop has missed. They think that the "immune system" which protects us from alien bacteria and other microbes can sometimes kill a cancer cell as well.

Other researchers think the answer is no. The body probably can't get rid of cancer cells. These scientists believe that once a single cancer cell has been formed, it will, in all likelihood, go on to grow into a cancer tumour. In their opinion, the immune system can only kill aliens, not cancer cells. While cancer cells are abnormal, they are too much like the normal cells in a person's body to be considered alien by the immune system.

To understand these two opposing theories, it's necessary to understand a little bit about the body's immune system which is made up of several parts. All of these parts work because cells — all cells — have various types of markers which sit on their surfaces. They are called "antigen" markers; I.D. cards is how Dr. Schachter describes them.

About 20 years ago, scientists discovered one type of antigen markers which they called "HLA markers" — human leukocyte markers. Ten genes, on the sixth chromosome of every human cell, produce 10 particular proteins which move to the surface of the cell where they sit, acting as an amazing self-identification system.

Every cell in your body has the exact same group of HLA markers. Any cell that doesn't belong to your body — a bit of bacteria, a virus, even a cell from another human — will not carry these unique identifying markers. They will carry 10 HLA markers, but they will be different from yours, and your body will perceive them as alien.

Around the same time, scientists also realized that cells have hundreds of other types of antigen markers sitting on their surface.

Before they had detected all these markers, scientists had also known for quite a long time that our bodies have a natural defence system, the immune system, that fights against disease. But once they were able to isolate these antigen markers, scientists realized that the immune system has several parts

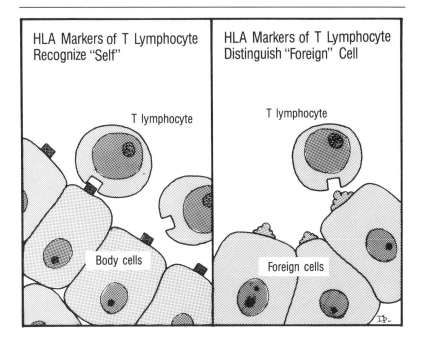

| HLA Markers of T Lymphocyte Recognize "Self" | HLA Markers of T Lymphocyte Distinguish "Foreign" Cell |

(Left panel: T lymphocyte, Body cells. Right panel: T lymphocyte, Foreign cells.)

and they began to figure out how each of these parts works.

One part of the immune system consists of certain white blood cells called "T lymphocytes" which are interested in the HLA antigen markers.

A second part of the immune system consists of white blood cells called "B lymphocytes" which are interested in the other types of antigen markers.

A third part of the immune system consists of white blood cells called "NK cells" — Natural Killer cells — which are interested in cells that have been attacked by viruses.

T lymphocytes are produced in the lymph nodes by certain blood stem cells. These immature cells are somehow influenced by a gland called the thymus, and they mature into T lymphocytes. In the lymph nodes of the lymphatic system — the system which keeps all the body's tissues bathed in fluid so they don't dry out — T lymphocytes are constantly on the lookout for anything that doesn't carry the 10 correct HLA markers. You can imagine these white blood cells sidling up to every cell that passes through and comparing notes. "Are your markers the same as my markers?"

If the markers are the same, fine. If they aren't, watch out. The white blood cells attach themselves to the intruder, and release certain chemicals which kill the offending cell.

B lymphocytes are also produced in the gastrointestinal tract by these blood stem cells. They start out as B cell lymphoblasts and, when they mature, they move into the lymphatic system. Eventually they mature further into plasma cells and are stored in the bone marrow.

B lymphocytes are on the lookout for anything that has foreign antigen markers on its surface. Each time the body senses the presence of a foreign antigen marker, B lymphocytes create "antibodies" that are designed specifically to recognize that foreign antigen.

These antibodies circulate through the body looking for their antigen mates. As soon as one of these antibodies spots the antigen for which it was created, it marks the cell that antigen is on. The cell is now cited for destruction: T lymphocytes come in and finish the job.

The third part of the immune system which is made up of NK cells, was discovered more recently than the other two parts. Scientists know much less about NK cells than either T or B lymphocytes, but they believe that NK cells can kill cells that have been invaded by viruses.

The theory is that NK cells work in conjunction with T lymphocyte cells. While a T lymphocyte cell is busy checking out a cell's HLA markers, it will also notice if a foreign bit of virus is stuck to the cell's surface. If it does notice a viral antigen marker, it will tell the body to produce Interferon, a chemical which can't actually kill virally-infected cells, but can at least keep them from reproducing. Interferon also stimulates NK cells to work harder than normal, and NK cells can kill cells that have been infected by a virus.

How Cancer Evades the Immune System

So why doesn't the immune system just kill a cell that somehow manages to mutate into a cancer cell? A cancer cell, after all, is a disease cell. It's alien, or in any case, it's certainly not normal, and it can do the body terrible harm.

Scientists like Dr. Schachter don't know the answer for certain. However, some of them do believe that one or more of the parts of the immune system can recognize and kill a few cancer cells, at least for a while. They believe that because cancer cells divide so quickly, they soon overpower the immune system; in almost no time at all, there might be too many cancer cells for the immune system to handle. They believe that research might come up with a way of strengthening the immune system to do a better job.

Other scientists believe that whatever caused the first cell to become cancerous might actually suppress the immune system, making it less able to work.

Still others believe that cancer cells themselves might actually produce something that prevents the immune system from working. Perhaps cancer cells do have markers that are different than normal cells, but can also disguise themselves in some way so that the white blood cells looking for unusual markers are fooled.

And still other scientists believe that only NK cells can kill cancer cells, but of course, NK cells would only respond to the rare cancer cells that have been mutated by viruses. This is one reason why so much research has been done with Interferon in recent years. Researchers have been trying to use the version of Interferon that they are able to produce in labs to stimulate NK cells to work better. They have injected cancer patients with Interferon and, in some cases, cancer tumours have shrunk. Unfortunately, the dream that some scientists had a few years ago of using Interferon to stimulate the immune system to fight all types of cancer has not yielded the results that had been hoped for. It may be that Interferon will work well on the rare cancers that are caused by viruses, but scientists aren't even certain about that.

"It may be," says Dr. Schachter, "that the immune system can't kill most types of cancer cells. It may be that cancer cells have the same HLA markers as normal cells and other antigen markers for which the body produces no antibodies — because the body does not consider these cancer cell antigens to be aliens." It makes sense.

"Don't forget," Dr. Schachter continues, "that a cancer cell, even though it's not functioning like a normal cell, came from a cell that was once normal. A cancer cell is not an alien, not an outsider. It's a cell from the person's own body. When you think of cancer cells that way, you can see how they might still have the right markers. While many things about a cell change when it becomes cancerous, it is possible that its markers don't change.

"It could also be that cancer cells don't have exactly the same markers as normal cells, but have some sort of protection on their cell surface. This protection could act as a disguise, enabling the cancer cell to *trick* the immune system into leaving it alone. That's another way to explain why the immune system may not kill cancer cells, why cancer cells go on dividing and dividing until eventually they form a tumour."

But that still leaves one thing about cancer left to explain — metastasis — the most deadly aspect of this deadly disease.

Because even if a gene does suffer damage and that damage escapes the first system that ordinarily repairs genes, only one cancer cell will be born. A single cancer cell is not going to hurt anybody very much.

And even if that one cancer cell does manage to escape the second control system — the immune system — and keeps dividing, only *one* cancer tumour will develop. While a cancerous tumour is extremely serious, and possibly fatal if it completely overpowers a vital organ, it would not be deadly in many, many cases *if it would only remain in the spot where it begins.*

The deadliest aspect of cancer is that it doesn't remain in one place. It spreads. Cells break off from the original tumour and metastasize to other organs where they form new tumours. How and why cancer cells can do this is one of the things that scientists understand least.

Says Dr. Schachter, "There must be another marker system, one that keeps control over where a cell may live. There must be, and it must be a marker system that the cancer cell can trick."

It's like an airplane that takes off from a foreign airport

on a scheduled flight — just a regular passenger flight, nothing suspicious. But then, after the plane takes off, it changes its route. It flies so low that it is not detected by radar, and it proceeds on a secret spy mission.

"It could be the same with a cancer cell," Dr. Schachter explains. "It could be that cancer cells trick this last fail-safe system too."

First one cancer cell would trick the immune system into letting it alone, and the first tumour forms. Then, a cell from this tumour breaks off and tricks this other system. It makes it through radar control, so to speak, and moves to a second organ where it sets up shop. Like the airplane that flies beneath the radar detection system, the cancer cell passes all the control systems. Eventually, it "hijacks" a third organ and then moves on to a fourth. In the end, there will be enough tumours to totally muck up the body's functions.

Some researchers, like Dr. Schachter, do believe that cancer cells probably have the same, or at least similar, markers as normal cells, or else some sort of protection which enables them to trick the immune system. They believe that if the markers on cancer cells were foreign, the immune system would notice a cancer cell and kill it.

But that doesn't happen with cancer. Cancer cells aren't killed; they grow. And unlike normal cells — which stick to their own kind, liver cell with liver cell, brain cell with brain cell — cancer cells can, and usually do, break off from the tumour. These "shed" cells then move, through the bloodstream or the lymphatic system, to other parts of the body. There they "seed" themselves, growing into new tumours, hijacking first one organ, then another, and eventually a third.

And the more cancer cells have spread, the harder they are to treat.

CHAPTER TWO

Who Gets Cancer and Who is at High Risk?

W HO gets cancer? The terrible truth is that cancer will strike 30 percent — almost one in three — of the people who are living in Canada today.

Cancer has been called a democratic disease. It knows no boundaries and plays no favourites; it can be found among people of all races and ages, both rich and poor, black and white, male and female. Cancer also strikes children, although fortunately, it is more common among older people.

One positive aspect of cancer is that it is definitely not contagious. Doctors, nurses, and researchers who treat cancer patients have no risk of catching this disease.

In fact, an unusual study was once done on prisoners who agreed to have cancer cells transplanted from cancer patients to their own healthy bodies. These transplants never worked. You can't get cancer by injecting cancer cells from one person into another. Neither can you get cancer from being around someone — even touching, or kissing someone — who has the disease.

And yet, when you know someone who has cancer, it is normal to start worrying about every bump, every pimple, every new bruise you discover on your own body. It's a terrible feeling that just about everyone has. You know that you may be over-reacting, but deep down inside, you are sure that you have cancer too. The fact is though, you almost certainly don't.

If someone in a family has cancer, chances are rarely greater that a second member of that family will get it. Chances are greater, in all but a few types of cancer, that someone from another family will develop the disease. That's just the way statistics work. The odds, just like in a game of dice, tend to get spread evenly around.

Still, it's scary, there's no denying that. Every year in Canada, almost 90,000 new cases of cancer are diagnosed; the disease has become more, not less, widespread in recent years.

In the 1930s, about one Canadian in six or seven got cancer at some point during his or her life. Now it is closer to one person in three.

But a closer look at the statistics reveals that the numbers are increasing, in part, because medicine has made so many advances. It sounds crazy at first, but think for a minute, and it will begin to make sense.

In 1930, the average lifespan was shorter. A lot of people died of pneumonia, influenza, tuberculosis, diptheria, and other diseases which medicine can now cure, or prevent by vaccination.

Prior to World War II, many young people died before reaching adolescence. Many of them would have gotten cancer if they had just lived long enough. Cancer, you see, is a disease which seems to affect people as they get older. It does strike children, but the average age of the 90,000 Canadians who are diagnosed with cancer each year is 64. Only 1,200 are under the age of 20 and only about 525 are under the age of 10. Almost all of these young people develop leukemia, Hodgkin's disease, cancer of the brain, or the type of bone cancer, called osteogenic sarcoma, that struck Terry Fox.

Among all Canadians under the age of 24, only one in 270 has had any type of cancer. The figures change for people between 24 and 55. Of those who didn't get cancer before age 24, one person in 17 will develop it before age 55. And one person in three who makes it to age 55 will end up with some form of the disease before age 75.

By the time you finish reading all these numbers, you may have the feeling that everyone ought to either have cancer or be on the verge of getting it. At first, the statistics look so negative, so grim. But the truth is, most people don't get cancer. More than two-thirds of all the people you will ever meet will not get this disease.

Of those who do get cancer, almost half won't die of it. And taking away lung cancer, which is one of the worst in terms of people actually dying, the figures look even better. Sixty percent of people who get some type of cancer, other than lung cancer, eventually die of something else. True, that "something else" is often old age, since many people are over 70-years-old when they develop cancer. When you look at the figures this way, they take on a different light.

Nevertheless, the big question which occupies the time of so many of today's researchers is WHO is likely to get cancer. Figures and bars and dotted lines are one thing; real people — some of whom we know and care about — are another.

Scientists called "epidemiologists" study groups of people who get a certain type of cancer and, often by a process of elimination, try to figure out what the cause of that cancer is and who has a higher-than-average risk of developing it. In recent years, a lot of research has been done to relate cancer to specific diets, particular chemicals, and high exposure to radiation and the ultraviolet rays of the sun.

Canadians and Americans, for example, use more fat in their diets than people of other countries in the world, and the rate of breast cancer and cancer of the colon are very high in North America. In Japan, Thailand, and India, people's diets are low in fat and these two types of cancer are comparatively rare. This finding has led epidemiologists to suggest that a high fat diet increases a person's risk of developing breast cancer and cancer of the colon.

On the other hand, researchers have also studied the incidence of cancer in countries where people's diets are low in fat. In some of these countries — and Japan is one of them — there seems to be a relationship between diet and other types of cancer.

While there is a low rate of cancer of the colon and breast cancer in Japan, stomach cancer is relatively high. In Canada, stomach cancer used to be high, but has been declining steadily over the past 30 years and is now relatively low. Epidemiologists believe that nutritional habits over many years affect a person's risk of developing stomach cancer. In fact, the dietary habits people acquire during their developmental years are thought by many researchers to sometimes be the cause of a cancer that shows up two or three decades later.

In Japan, people eat a lot of foods preserved with nitrates and nitrites, as well as a lot of smoked foods. They also tend to eat very little of the fresh fruits and vegetables that contain high amounts of vitamin C. These were also the habits of Canadians until, in the 1940s, refrigeration became more accessible to the average person. Many epidemiologists believe that foods containing nitrates and nitrites contribute to stomach cancer while vitamin C actually protects people against it. They use this explanation to account for the high rate of stomach cancer in Japan and the declining rate of this disease here in Canada.

But what about the two and a half million people who live in a city like Toronto? Epidemiologists can compare the people of Canada to the people of Japan pretty easily when they are talking about differences in diet.

When they are looking at who among the people of one city are likely to get cancer, however, epidemiologists must take other factors into consideration. They can still talk about diet, for example, but the issue becomes more difficult to sort out. They must also add other factors, like chemicals, to the discussion and these come under the general heading of lifestyle. Some of the lifestyle factors that increase a person's risk of developing cancer are ones that they themselves choose, such as smoking. Other factors, like exposure to certain chemicals, have less to do with individual choice and more to do with the environment or a person's occupation.

Let's have another look at diet and its relationship to cancer. Canada is a multicultural society. Many people have immigrated to Canada from other countries, but these people usually stick to the dietary habits they had in their homelands.

The people who have moved to Canada from Japan are a good example. It is not surprising that the people who live in Canada now, but grew up in Japan, would have a higher rate of stomach cancer than Canadians. These people have been affected by the high nitrate/nitrite, low vitamin C diets they had as children in Japan. The children of Japanese immigrants — children who were actually born in Canada, not Japan — also have a higher rate of stomach cancer. This may seem surprising, but according to most epidemiologists, the answer is still likely diet. Because of their cultural heritage, people carry on the dietary habits of their parents, at least for a generation or two. The third generation of Japanese-Canadians, however, tends to drift away from their grand-parents' type of diet toward the dietary habits of non-immigrant Canadians. They have the same rate of stomach cancer as the rest of the population.

People of other cultural backgrounds also tend to develop certain types of cancer more or less frequently because of dietary habits that can change when they move. For example, when many Eastern Europeans migrated to Canada, they traded their low fat diets for the high fat diets of North Americans. As they did this, their incidence of breast cancer and cancer of the colon increased.

Yet diet is only one factor. Take two people who were born in Toronto, whose parents were born in Toronto, and who have always followed the same dietary habits. Why does one person develop cancer and not the other?

Lifestyle may be the answer. The most obvious example of a chosen lifestyle which increases the risk of developing cancer is cigarette smoking. Scientists have been able to show that all other things being equal, a person who starts smoking cigarettes at age 15 is 30 times more likely to develop lung cancer at age 35 than someone who has never smoked.

Epidemiologists have also been able to show that about 30 chemicals — vinyl chloride which is used in the manufacture of aerosol sprays and plastics, is one example — are carcinogenic to people. People who have worked with vinyl chloride over a period of many years are more likely to develop cancer of the liver than other people. Fortunately, there are now guidelines for using vinyl chloride in a way that ensures the safety of workers.

Inhaling asbestos fibres is something else that can lead to lung cancer 10 or 20 years down the road. And a smoker who works with asbestos is far more likely to develop lung cancer than a non-smoker who works with asbestos. As with vinyl chloride, guidelines have been issued for the use of asbestos, although some researchers argue that they are not tough enough.

It is true, however, that you can find two people of the same cultural heritage who live in the same city, have very similar lifestyles, and the same type of job with the same exposure to harmful chemicals, and still one will develop cancer and the other will not.

This is a mystery that some researchers believe will someday be able to be explained and that every individual will be able to be assessed and have his or her particular risk factors pinpointed. Research into genetics and immunology has been going on for 10 years and, already, there have been some remarkable and fascinating discoveries.

Some theories suggest that a person may be more sensitive to cancer at one time in his or her life than at another time. And that some people are simply more sensitive to cancer than other people — period.

How could it really be that someone might be more sensitive to cancer at one time in his or her life than at another? One explanation has to do with age; as people get older, they may become more susceptible to cancer. Another explanation has to do with cell division. If a person's cells start dividing more frequently than usual — and that can happen at any age for any number of reasons — then the simple law of averages says that the genes in those cells have more chances of becoming mutated. This is especially true if the cells are being bombarded by a carcinogen during the period of rapid division.

Consider the aging theory. By the time people are older, they have had more opportunities to be exposed to carcinogens. Also, the mechanisms in an old body begin to wear out. Eighty-year-old knees don't bend as well as they did at age 25. By the same token, researchers suggest that old surveillance systems might wear out as well. The repair shop that watches out for genetic errors during cell division might not be as efficient as it once was. The immune system may wear down and not recognize antigen markers as well; NK cells may not respond to Interferon or, perhaps, less Interferon is produced. Perhaps the system which prevents cells from metastasizing doesn't work quite as well either.

Scientists don't have answers for these questions. They do know that the average age of cancer patients is 64, and from this, they theorize that older people may be more susceptible to cancer.

It is frightening to think that during some periods of life a person might be more sensitive to a carcinogen than during other periods. But if you think about how and when cells divide, this too will begin to make sense.

Remember the example of an Indian corn seed being planted by mistake in a row of regular corn seeds? Well, when a cell is dividing, it is more sensitive to a carcinogen than when it is not dividing. It follows, then, that if cells in a particular organ start dividing rapidly — far more rapidly than is normal — there will be more chances for a gene to make an error. The more errors that are made, the harder it is for the genetic repair shop to keep up.

Imagine a table fan on a desk on a hot summer day. If the fan is turned off and its blades are just turning a little in the breeze, you could throw a wrench into the fan and do very little damage. But turn the fan on high speed, and then throw in a wrench. The blades would look like spaghetti in a second.

But why would your cells be dividing more quickly at one time in your life than at another? Why would they ever be dividing so quickly that the repair shop couldn't keep up?

If a lot of cells suddenly die for one reason or another, then a lot of rapid cell division would be necessary to replace them. Normally cell division occurs relatively slowly. A cell dies. It is replaced. Another one dies, it is replaced.

It is true that some cells, such as blood cells, multiply very quickly compared with other cells, such as liver cells. But as far as the blood cells' reproduction system is concerned, their normal rate of division isn't too fast for the genetic repair shop to keep up. This system is meant to work quickly and few errors escape the repair shop's eagle eye.

Other systems are not designed to work as quickly. One time that cells could be dividing too quickly for the repair shop to keep up is when skin becomes sunburned.

If you sunbathe without using a sunscreen, your skin will burn. You can actually see it happen! When skin gets sunburned, the body must make new skin cells. Millions of skin cells die all at once and they must be replaced quickly. There is more cell division going on which makes it more difficult for the genetic repair shop to keep up with any errors that might occur. And to make matters worse, while this quick division is going on, more carcinogenic ultraviolet rays are hitting the skin cells.

Another example is a person with a lung infection such as bronchitis. When someone has bronchitis, the lungs become inflamed, meaning that a lot of lung cells have died. To replace those that have been lost, lung cells begin dividing quickly. Again, it is difficult for the lung's genetic repair shop to keep up.

Now, imagine that while this rapid cell division is going on, a person is also smoking. The chances that the cigarette smoke will damage a gene in a lung cell are greater while the lung cells are dividing like crazy. The law of averages also says that the chances are greater that a growth gene will happen to be affected. If one is, a cancer cell will be born.

The other theory suggests that some people might simply be more sensitive to cancer-causing substances than other people — not just on certain occasions, but all the time.

The most obvious explanation for this is that one person's repair system might not work as well as another person's, regardless of age and lifestyle.

After all, Steve Podborski is a better skier, and Karen Kain is a better dancer than most people no matter how hard those other people try. Maybe one person's T and B lymphocyte cells are just better at recognizing subtle differences in HLA markers and other antigen markers than another person's.

Although scientists don't know for sure, some believe that even the system which prevents metastasis may work better in one person's body than in another person's, even though they are the same age. That would explain why similar cancer tumours sometimes spread, or metastasize, more quickly in one person than in another.

All these theories are being investigated by researchers, and already some interesting experiments have taken place.

People with red hair and light skin tend to get skin cancer more often than people with brown hair and darker skin. Why? Probably because the red-haired person's skin burns more easily. Light skin contains less of a substance called "melanin" which protects skin cells from the ultraviolet rays of the sun and carcinogenic chemicals in the environment.

Since red-haired, light skinned people burn more easily, their skin cells would be damaged sooner than dark-haired, darker skinned people's skin cells. Because redheads' skin cells are dividing rapidly for longer, there are simply more opportunities for damage to be done.

Some explanations are more complex than the amount of melanin in someone's skin. Lung cancer has been directly linked to cigarette smoking. Of the 9,600 Canadians who develop lung cancer each year, few are non-smokers. But why is it that many smokers don't get lung cancer? Why one person, but not another? Why your dad, but not mine?

An explanation by Dr. Zsolt Harsanyi, an American scientist who, with writer Richard Hutton, co-authored the book *Genetic Prophecy: Beyond the Double Helix* suggests that there might be something about one person's lung cells that make him or her more susceptible to lung cancer.

According to Dr. Harsanyi, when you inhale smoke from a cigarette, you get a bunch of different chemicals in your lungs. Some of these chemicals are perfectly harmless. The lungs dissolve them and they are carried to the kidneys by the bloodstream. In the kidneys, they are processed some more and then they leave the body as waste.

But other chemicals in cigarette smoke are not as easily dissolved. What's worse, they are actually poisonous. Some, like tars, also become carcinogenic when they are chemically altered even slightly.

The lungs won't tolerate poisons which could eventually build up to what are called "toxic" levels that could cause death. In their desire to clean themselves, they try to get rid of these poisons. Certain genes in certain lung cells produce specific proteins, called enzymes, which turn these poisons into substances that can be dissolved in the bloodstream. Once in the bloodstream, these poisons can travel to the kidneys to be disposed of once and for all.

One particular group of undissolvable poisons in cigarette smoke are tars called polycyclic hydrocarbons. These tars can become carcinogens with only minor chemical changes.

A special group of enzymes, produced by a special group of genes, works on these hydrocarbons to get them into a form that can be dissolved in the bloodstream.

Dr. Harsanyi describes these enzymes as if they were workers in a factory assembly line. Each gene, or factory worker, makes an enzyme that either adds to, or chops off, a different part of a hydrocarbon. With each step, the hydrocarbon gets a little closer to a dissolvable form.

Now it happens that one of these enzymes — one that works somewhere in the middle of the chain — is called AHH, which stands for aryl hydrocarbon hydroxylase. The problem with AHH is that while it does make a hydrocarbon more dissolvable, it also changes it into a carcinogen.

Normally, if the body is working well and all the factory worker genes are in tune with one another, this cancer-causing stage doesn't last very long. The next factory worker in the line comes along and converts the hydrocarbon still further — into a substance that is no longer cancer-causing.

But suppose the gene in the assembly line that produces the AHH enzyme is overactive. If that happens, then the next gene in the chain won't be able to keep up. The hydrocarbon will get to the cancer-causing stage in the chain and remain there for a relatively long period of time.

The more cancer-causing substances that are produced, and the longer they stay around, the more likely it is that they will damage a gene. If they happen to cause a growth gene to mutate into an oncogene, a cancer cell will be born.

But just as scientists ask why some people have light skin that produces low amounts of melanin, they ask why other people have a gene that produces too much AHH.

They ask, but at the moment, they can't answer. It's like asking why some people are tall and others are short. It has to do with heredity. Why one child will inherit one particular trait and another child in the same family will not, is another of the amazing mysteries of life — and, perhaps, the luck of the draw.

It's easy to see who has light skin and is therefore more sensitive to skin cancer, but just finding a gene that produces too much AHH is tricky, and very expensive. There are very few genetic research centres with the gene-slicing equipment necessary to begin studying genes. Even fewer of these laboratories are concerned with cancer. It's not possible for a family doctor doing a check-up to analyze genes. And it's unlikely that this situation will change in the near future.

Still, some scientists hope that if enough money is put into this type of genetic research, significant progress will be made.

Someday, scientists may develop a simple, inexpensive way to determine whether one person is more sensitive to the poisons in cigarette smoke than another person because of basic genetic differences. For all smokers, the chances of developing lung cancer are one in 10. But imagine if scientists could narrow the risk for certain people to one in three, or one in two. Imagine if they could tell a person, ''Look, if *you* smoke, given the way your genes are, it will be amazing if you *don't* get lung cancer.'' Imagine that!

At the moment, it can't be done; not with lung cancer anyway. But scientists are starting to identify other genes that seem to point to certain types of cancer.

Scientists have learned that retinoblastoma, a rare form of eye cancer that affects children under the age of four, is one of the few types of cancer that tends to occur in the brothers and sisters of children with this disease. They also know that retinoblastoma is due to a genetic abnormality — the absence of a number of genes on a person's thirteenth chromosome. Doctors will therefore watch the brothers and sisters of retinoblastoma patients very carefully, and will usually be able to detect the disease at an early stage when it can be cured without the child having to lose an eye. Looking for answers to medical questions through genetics is starting to become more and more common.

Researchers are also beginning to link genetic abnormalities to other, more common kinds of cancer. Breast cancer and cancer of the kidney are among the ones that are now being investigated.

Our hope for the future in this type of research is almost limitless. It might mean that some day, doctors could warn a person to watch out for a certain type of cancer, or a certain cancer-causing chemical to which he or she might be particularly susceptible. Not only would our society have a general knowledge about things that increase the risk of cancer, but each person would have his or her own special risk-factor scheme.

What we are talking about, of course, is prevention; the idea that the best cure for cancer may be making sure that people don't get it at all.

CHAPTER THREE
Prevention

I N 1960, American President John F. Kennedy announced that there would be a person on the moon before the end of the decade. You know what? Kennedy was making a safe bet. He knew it was possible. Succeeding was only a matter of hard work and money.

The rockets existed; they just weren't powerful enough. The materials for space suits existed; they just weren't tough enough. What was needed were some adjustments to what already existed, rather than something completely new. By 1960, a craft had already been put into space. Getting one onto the moon, with an astronaut in it, was a matter of doing the same thing scientists already knew how to do, only better. It happened, of course, in the summer of 1969.

Finding the ultimate cure for cancer, however, is not like getting astronaut Neil Armstrong onto the moon. Another American president, Richard M. Nixon, found that out after he announced, in 1972, that Americans would find a way to eradicate cancer from the face of the earth by the beginning of the 1980s.

The fact that President Nixon's dream still hasn't been realized is nobody's fault. Finding the ultimate cure to cancer is a lot tougher to achieve than putting a person on the moon. As Dr. Schachter explained, finding that cure involves understanding the cause of cancer at a cellular level, and that involves learning the answers to some basic cellular principles about which scientists are just beginning to gain some understanding.

And yet, in spite of all the depressing figures about the number of deaths from cancer each year, a lot is happening in the field of cancer research that is positive. One of the most positive developments is in the area of prevention — preventing cancer through an examination of our environment. The word environment is meant to include diet, as well as chemicals, radiation, and viruses.

Right now, with the knowledge scientists already have, cancer can often be prevented. In fact, some researchers believe that cancer is preventable as much as 80 or 90 percent of the time. These researchers believe that although we don't know the basics of how cancer begins, we do know many of its environmental causes, most of which are within our control.

Dr. Tony Miller, director of epidemiology for the National Cancer Institute of Canada, has broken the causes of cancer into four groups. Diet, he believes, accounts for between 35 and 50 percent of all cancers. He emphasizes, however, that this field is complex, and that researchers have not yet sorted out all the relationships between cancer and food.

Chemicals, Dr. Miller believes, account for approximately 40 percent of all cancers, but only about five percent of those are chemicals other than cigarette smoke. Radiation and viruses, he says, account for another three, or four, percent of all cancers. If you add all these percentages, you get approximately 93 percent; only six percent of cancers remain unaccounted for.

When faced with statistics such as these, many people agree with Dr. Miller that prevention is the most important area of cancer research. They believe that as much money should be spent on prevention — learning more about the exact environmental causes of cancer and educating more people to consider them — as is spent on other types of research and treatment. At the moment, relatively little of the money raised by the Canadian Cancer Society is earmarked for prevention. Nevertheless, while "basic" researchers, and "applied" researchers continue to work on basic answers, and ways of applying these answers to patients, epidemiological researchers, like Dr. Miller, continue their work in the area of prevention, uncovering more and more answers to cancer's environmental links.

The concept of cancer prevention began 200 years ago when Dr. Percival Pott noticed that many of his scrotal cancer patients had worked as chimney sweeps when they were young boys — too many for the high incidence to be merely coincidental. Although the science, or even the word epidemiology, had not yet been invented, Dr. Pott was the world's first epidemiologist.

It seemed like a good idea to think about why so many chimney sweeps were developing cancer of the scrotum, and so Dr. Pott began asking his patients details about their lives. Many told him that as children sweeping chimneys, they had rarely washed or changed their soot-stained clothes. They said they had been too poor to afford more than one set of clothing, and bathtubs were not exactly the norm in the 1700s. Dr. Pott theorized that over the years, the powerful carcinogens in the burned coal were being absorbed into the chimney sweeps' skin. These carcinogens, he believed, were causing scrotal cancer to appear decades later.

While Dr. Pott was astute enough to look at the statistics and realize that something in soot must be causing the scrotal cancer, the Danes were the first people to practise cancer prevention as a nation. They passed a law which stated that all chimney sweeps had to wash and change their soot-stained clothes every day after work. When the number of cases of scrotal cancer began to decline in Denmark, other nations began to follow suit.

It was not, however, for almost 200 years that the most important discovery in cancer prevention was made. In the early 1950s, the first articles linking cigarettes to the most deadly cancer of all, lung cancer, appeared in American and British scientific journals. Over the next few years, more articles appeared. Then, in 1962, the British Royal College of Physicians published a report on smoking and health. In 1964, the U.S. Surgeon General did the same. Both reports stated that the chance of developing lung cancer increases with the number of cigarettes a person smokes.

"Up until 1964," says Dr. David Nostbakken, national director of public education for the Canadian Cancer Society, "the smoking public puffed away, unaware of the health hazard. There was, I suppose, a general feeling that smoking wasn't exactly *good* for you. But the real evidence that conclusively links cigarettes to cancer was not known when our parents were teenagers. Many people have lung cancer today because they became addicted to cigarettes during the years when we were all still so naive. Now that we do know, however, we could eventually prevent a third of all cancer deaths . . . if we could only convince young people not to start smoking.''

You'd think it would be easy to convince teenagers not to smoke. Studies show that a teenager who begins smoking a pack-a-day at age 15 is 30 times more likely to develop lung cancer by age 35 than one who has never smoked. And yet, studies also indicate that the age at which teenagers are starting to smoke has actually gone down, from 15 years to 12.

How can this be? People like Dr. Nostbakken blame the tobacco companies with their multimillion dollar advertising campaigns; in Canada alone, the tobacco industry spends one hundred million dollars a year — $100,000,000 — trying to promote smoking as both sophisticated and healthy. According to Dr. Nostbakken, young Canadians fall for these kinds of ads.

The tobacco companies insist that they are not interested in trying to convince young people to smoke. They claim that the purpose of their advertising dollars is merely to get smokers to change brands — as if even *that* would be ethical. Meanwhile, each time I look at another new ad which pictures smoking hand in hand with sophistication — and even sports — I become more and more sceptical about trusting these claims.

In 1984, when tobacco manufacturer RJR-Macdonald Inc. began to sponsor the Canadian Ski Association with the ''Export A Cup'' there was no longer any doubt in my mind. If tobacco companies are really not interested in getting young Canadians to smoke, why are they so keen to spend five million dollars sponsoring ski events where the majority of participants, and fans, are under 18? Why do all their ads suggest that young people who live the good life always smoke?

The answer is simple. Tobacco companies are not in business to lose money. They are in business to sell tobacco to whomever they can convince to buy it and they couldn't care less if that person is 16 or 86.

Dispelling the sophisticated image of smoking is tackled by the Canadian Cancer Society and a few other organizations. Unfortunately, they have only a few million dollars a year to spend. Until there is more money for this purpose, Canadians will probably continue to spend more than five billion dollars a year on cigarettes and close to two billion dollars on health care because of cigarettes. Close to 10,000 Canadians a year will continue to develop lung cancer. And because lung cancer is almost always impossible to treat, close to the same number will die. It's a bitter-sweet notion that we know how to prevent lung cancer, but don't

Skin cancer is another type of cancer we know how to prevent, but don't. Every year in Canada, almost 17,000 new cases of skin cancer are diagnosed, mostly because of over- exposure to the ultraviolet rays of the sun without the protection of a sunscreen.

Many people overexpose themselves to sunshine because of tough-to-resist advertising. In this case, the ads try to make us believe that suntans are beautiful and, ironically enough, healthy!

It is lucky that skin cancer is not the killer that lung cancer is. Almost all of the 17,000 people who develop skin cancer each year can be cured.

In other cases, however, people have applied the knowledge about prevention that epidemiologists have come up with. For example, luminous watch paint that glows in the dark contains radium and has been linked to bone cancer. Sixty years ago, factory workers used this type of paint to draw numbers on watches. They dipped their brushes into the paint and, to get a fine point, tipped them against their tongues.

Obviously, these workers were swallowing a certain amount of the paint, and although no one was aware of it, the radium in it was settling in their bones. When many of these workers developed bone cancer, the connection was eventually made, the practice stopped, and the incidence of bone cancer declined.

Over the years, scientists have learned other things about the relationship between radiation and cancer. Twenty-five years ago, for example, children who were being fitted for shoes stuck their feet into radiation machines which outlined the toes to show how the shoes fit. I can remember giggling at the picture of my own toes squiggling inside a "magic" machine.

Since Dr. Percival Pott identified soot as a carcinogen, about 30 additional chemicals have been shown to cause cancer in humans. Many of them are now avoided. You may not be old enough to recall the feet machines, but you may remember when newspaper articles about the cancer-causing properties of asbestos started to appear. Before the early 1970s, asbestos was commonly used as a building material because it was both fire-proof and an excellent insulator. When scientists realized that asbestos is also a powerful carcinogen, its use was reduced.

Other chemicals which we now avoid — or at least use carefully — include vinyl chloride, the cleaning fluid carbon tetrachloride, and a type of solvent called benzene.

Identifying carcinogenic chemicals is only one of many areas of cancer prevention. Scientists have also developed tests which can detect cancer in its very early stages. In these cases, they are not able to prevent cancer completely, but they are able to prevent it from becoming a life-threatening disease.

Most of the time, for instance, death from cervical cancer can be prevented because it can be detected at a very early stage. This is due to the work of a Greek doctor, George Papanicoulaou, who invented the Pap test, a simple, painless procedure which takes less than a minute for a doctor to perform.

A swab of cells from the cervix — it's as easy as scraping a few cells from the inside of your cheek — are smeared onto a piece of glass and then studied in the lab. From the way the cells look, cancer can be detected at its earliest stage and cured completely *before* it progresses. It's an amazing preventive technique that has saved the lives of thousands of women around the world.

Scientists have also learned, for example, that people who develop polyps — tiny growths in the colon — have a higher-than-average-risk of developing cancer of the colon, *if* these non-cancerous polyps are not treated. Now, a careful watch is kept on these patients, and their polyps are removed before any cancerous changes have had a chance to take place.

Inroads are being made for breast cancer as well. There are now several ways of detecting breast cancer at an early stage, the easiest being breast self-examination — BSE. Studies have shown that women who know how to do BSE properly can detect early breast tumours that are no larger than a pea. On the other hand, breast tumours discovered by accident have often grown to the size of a golf ball. Death from breast cancer can be prevented 85 percent of the time if it is detected at an early stage. Today, more and more women are being diagnosed with breast cancer at this early stage.

Very little is heard about stomach cancer anymore. In the last chapter, I mentioned that the decline in the incidence of this disease has to do with the decline in the use of preservatives such as nitrates and nitrites, and the increase in the use of fresh fruit and vegetables, particularly those that are high in vitamin C. Epidemiologists are responsible for our knowledge of nitrates, nitrites, and vitamin C. In Canada, in 1930, 24 new cases of stomach cancer were reported each year for every 100,000 people. Today, in 1984, there are only about nine cases per 100,000 people.

Recently, researchers have come up with even more information about cancer prevention, information that links certain types of cancer to certain types of food. What remains to be seen is whether or not we will use this knowledge. It will mean changing our dietary habits — the lifestyle we have become accustomed to over the past 30 or 40 years.

A high fat diet increases a person's risk of developing cancer of the colon and the rectum, cancer of the prostate in men, and breast cancer in women. The Canadian Cancer Society, which has always been cautious about linking diet to cancer, is now suggesting that the average Canadian could reduce his or her risk of developing cancer by dietary changes.

They are advising us to eat less fat: no more than 30 percent of the calories consumed daily should be made up of fat. This means cutting down on fatty meats and whole milk products: cream; ice cream; and high fat yogurt. An interesting study on animals that is in no way conclusive for humans suggests that the fat contained in meats may have a more adverse affect than the fat contained in milk products. More studies in this area are being conducted.

To cut down on their fat intake, people must replace high fat products with other foods. High fibre content foods such as fruit, vegetables, and whole grains are recommended. These may even decrease a person's risk of developing cancer although scientists' opinions on this issue are still divided.

A diet rich in vitamins C and A is thought to decrease the risk of developing certain types of cancer.

Vitamin C is thought to protect humans against stomach cancer and cancer of the esophagus, probably because it neutralizes the effects of preservatives such as nitrates and nitrites. In fact, many of the foods preserved with nitrates and nitrites now contain vitamin C as well.

The information so far on vitamin A, which is also called carotene, is sketchier. Studies done on animals, and a few on humans, suggest that vitamin A may lower the risk of cancer of the larynx, esophagus, and lung. Carrots contain vitamin A as do apricots, cantaloupes, tomatoes, spinach, and peaches.

Scientists point out, however, that popping vitamin A supplements is not a good idea since excessive amounts of this vitamin can be toxic. I went to school with a guy who, after six weeks of eating nothing but carrots and vitamin A supplements, turned an amazing shade of orange. As they carted him home from the hospital after tests, the doctor said he had overdosed on carotene!

Dr. Miller also points out that while spinach contains vitamin C, it also contains nitrates. If you're interested in getting out of eating spinach, you might want to mention this epidemiological point!

Some research has suggested that "brassica" type vegetables, such as cabbage, broccoli, brussels sprouts, cauliflower, and kohlrabi, may reduce the risk of cancer of the colon and cancer of the rectum. That's because brassica vegetables contain certain impossible-to-pronounce chemicals such as isothiocynates, indoles, flavones, and phenols.

Heavy drinkers of alcohol, especially those who also smoke,

have an unusually high risk of developing oral cancer as well as a disease of the liver called cirrhosis, which sometimes leads to liver cancer. Researchers believe that something in the distillation process of alcohol causes it to become carcinogenic, to a minor degree. The Canadian Cancer Society is recommending that people drink alcohol in moderation.

Moderation is also the word where smoked and salt-cured foods, as well as nitrates and nitrites, are concerned. The amount of nitrate and nitrite that can, by law, be used as preservatives was reduced some years ago. Hams, fish, and some types of sausage which are still smoked in the traditional way absorb cancer-causing tars during the smoking process that are similar to the ones found in cigarette smoke. There is also some evidence linking salt-cured or pickled food to cancer of the stomach and esophagus.

Can we change our diets? The recommendations to eat more fruits and vegetables that contain vitamin C and vitamin A, whole grains, and fewer processed foods, should be fairly easy habits to assimilate. The recommendation to drink alcohol moderately will probably be the same as it has always been — easy for some people, difficult for others.

Reducing the amount of fat in our diets could cause problems. Already there have been some noises from certain Canadian industries which, like the tobacco industry, have a great deal at stake. The dairy industry, for example, could transfer some of its profits from whole milk and high fat yogurt to skim milk, and to low fat yogurt. But what about ice cream? And what about the beef industry? On certain cuts of beef, it is difficult to trim fat away. Some researchers are worried that the beef industry, which doesn't make huge profits to begin with, may not feel like taking this latest health edict lying down.

In the end, will we, as a society, change our eating habits? Or will a political battle similar to the one launched by the tobacco companies emerge? It's hard to say, since beef-eaters, or milkshake-lovers, don't ruin the environment for others in the same way as smokers can ruin the environment of their non-smoking friends.

In any case, the answer to whether or not 35 to 50 percent of cancer will someday be prevented through dietary changes is not in the hands of adults. This question will be answered in the future by teenagers like you who are old enough to make new choices.

And as you get older, epidemiologists will likely discover even more about cancer prevention. Like the science of genetics, the study of cancer and diet is a relatively new field. As well, thousands of new chemicals are developed each year and each must be tested to determine if it has carcinogenic properties.

One thing, however, is clear. Prevention, like basic research, is an exciting field. If we already have the knowledge to prevent approximately 80 percent of all cancer, who would want to argue that going further in the area of epidemiology and education is less important than discovering a cellular cure.

CHAPTER FOUR

Treatment — Living with Cancer

L EARNING about prevention is exciting for people who don't have cancer, or don't know someone who does. Learning about genes and what a deeper knowledge of their function could mean someday in terms of eradicating cancer, is exciting too. But today, this very year, almost 90,000 Canadians have found out that they have cancer. What is happening to them?

Most of them are being treated by one of the several hundred "oncologists" who work in Canadian hospitals. Oncologists are doctors who specialize in cancer treatment. The "onco" part of the word comes from the same Greek word as the "onco" in oncogene: *onkos* means tumour, or mass.

Dr. Richard Hasselback is one of these oncologists. He treats cancer patients at the Princess Margaret Hospital in Toronto where he has been working for 22 years. He is well aware of the truth: that treatment will be successful for fewer than half of the people who become cancer patients this year.

But Dr. Hasselback has also seen some exciting advances over the years. And he knows that five years from now — five is the numbers of years it takes until most types of cancer are considered "cured" — almost 45,000 of those 90,000 Canadians will be among the more than half a million Canadians who have fought cancer and won.

Matthew is one of these people. Six years ago, a doctor extracted a sample of blood from a vein in Matthew's left arm, sent it to a lab, and got back a report indicating an abnormal number of white blood cells. The next day, Matthew was hospitalized for a "bone marrow aspiration" test to see if his blood-producing cells — his blood stem cells — were cancerous. They were. The diagnosis was acute leukemia, cancer of the white cells of the blood. At the time, Matthew was 38. He was married to Diana and they had three children. Aubrey was 14; Lillian was eight; and little Sol was only three.

Matthew: "It happened just before Christmas. There was no snow that year." Even now it takes Matthew a few moments to build up to talking about his experience with cancer. "I had been exhausted for weeks. I didn't want Diana to worry, so I went to see Jack, our family doctor, on my own. Hell, it was probably nothing. But I think now, in my heart, I must have known."

The next two days were a tornado. Matthew had the blood test and then the bone marrow aspiration. An oncologist was called in and his treatment with chemicals — "chemotherapy" they call it — was started the same night.

Certain things about the three most often used treatments for cancer have changed over the years. But in many ways, they are the same basic treatments that physicians like Dr. Hasselback had to choose from 20 years ago: surgery, radiation therapy, and chemotherapy (which is used far more often today than in the past).

Matthew: "Treatment! I didn't think about treatment. I don't think it even crossed my mind that my chances were less than 50-50, that the drugs they were pumping into my veins were the only thing between me and death. All I could think about was Diana and the kids. How in the world was this going to affect them?"

Aubrey, the oldest, remembers the night when Matthew was hooked up to the intravenous tube, the I.V., that would deliver those drugs: "I'd never seen him like that before. He was so . . . twitchy . . . I can't think of any other word. I was there, you know, for half an hour and he kept going on about the weather and my school. It was crazy. Mom had said he had something really important to tell us. I mean, you don't exactly go into the hospital for the good of your health!" Aubrey pauses for a few seconds for emphasis. He looks pleased with himself for making the little joke. Six years ago, however, joking around was a little harder.

Matthew: "Kids have this idea about their parents. Hell, I'm 44 now and I still have the same fantasy about my own mom and dad. You think that because parents are adults, they can handle these crises without cracking up. I'm a pretty open guy. I believe in sharing my feelings with my family. But I can tell you, I felt about six-years-old the night I had to tell my kids.

"I remember hearing myself blurt it out after what seemed like hours of talking about nothing. Saying the word 'cancer' was the hardest part of all. After that, telling them that it was leukemia, and that I might die, didn't seem very hard."

Aubrey: "Yup, so that was it. He finally worked up to saying it: cancer. What did I know about cancer? But, you know, when he said it, suddenly, I figured it would be okay. I think now, looking back, it was that he finally trusted us enough to say it. I never thought he would die."

When you start to talk about whether a person with cancer will live or die — and it is a horrible thing to think of someone you love as part of a winning or losing group — you have to talk about many, many things. One of them, of course, is which kind of cancer that person has.

Almost no one with skin cancer or lip cancer, for example, dies of their disease. These are not the most serious kinds of cancer in the sense that they are almost always discovered early, treated, and cured.

At the other end are lung cancer, liver cancer, and cancer of the pancreas. Very few of the people with one of these types of cancer make it to the end of those critical first five years. The reasons are complicated. But basically, cancers like these are so hard to cure because they are "asymptomatic" in their early stages; that is, there are no signs or symptoms. Because of this, they are rarely discovered before they have advanced too far to be treated successfully.

Most of the other types of cancer are in the middle of these two extremes. Breast cancer, some types of leukemia, cancers of the lymphatic system, cancers of the bone, the uterus, the rectum, and the colon are all in a huge grey area. When a person is diagnosed with one of these kinds of cancer, the outcome can almost always go either way. Living in this grey area, sometimes for years, can be one of the most difficult aspects of cancer with which people must cope.

But another even more stressful aspect to cancer treatment is a general statement which cancer patients, or their families, often hear: that the *overall success rate* for treatment has not changed all that much over the past 30 years.

Is the statement true? Yes and no is how Dr. Hasselback explains it: "It's true, but the main reason why the overall figures for cancer treatment have not changed over the past 30 years has to do with lung cancer.

"The death rate for cancer of the colon is down — although only slightly.

"Breast cancer has stayed the same, but you can say that we are doing better with the *treatment* of breast cancer in one sense. More women are developing breast cancer today than in the past. Nevertheless, about the same number of women are dying of it each year. This means that in more cases, the treatment is successful.

"Deaths from certain types of leukemia, Hodgkin's disease, testicular cancer, thyroid cancer, stomach cancer, and cancer of the cervix have declined dramatically. Successes have come because of treatment for the first four, because of prevention in the case of stomach cancer, and because of early discovery in the case of cancer of the cervix.

"But lung cancer . . . ." Dr. Hasselback's voice remains steady, but it's not difficult to get a sense of how he feels. "If it weren't for the fact that the number of people who get lung cancer and die from it keeps going up, the overall cure rate for cancer would be improving, not staying the same."

Dr. Miller confirms what Dr. Hasselback has to say. "If lung cancer were wiped out — that is, if cigarettes were suddenly obliterated from the face of the earth — the number of deaths from lung cancer would all but stop, and deaths from cancer in general would eventually decline by a third."

The picture is fairly black and white when you talk about the easy-to-treat cancers on the one hand, and the almost impossible-to-treat ones on the other. But the discussion of survival and death is a much more complicated matter for most other types of cancer.

Often, when cancer is first detected, it is impossible for the doctors to say for certain if a particular person will live or die.

Matthew: "How can I even begin to describe what I thought about life and death during those first few weeks? Would the anti-cancer chemicals they were shooting into me kill my cancer cells, or would my cancer cells kill me? One minute I was sure I'd live. The next minute I'd figure I'd had it. . . . I tried so hard not to take out the anger and self-pity I felt about being in this shitty position on Diana and the kids. But I know there were many times when I failed. They all tell me now that I mostly said I was sorry when I jumped on them for nothing. But sometimes I wonder if they just say it to make me feel a little better."

Aubrey: "It's true. A lot of the time during that first month he was a yo-yo — up one day, down the next. I think we all were. One day I'd understand why he was in a bad mood and sympathize. I knew the drugs were making him sick as a dog and that he was scared half to death. But the next day I'd think, 'Do I need this? Here I am giving up my weekends to sit here with him. The least he can do is appreciate me.' "

Matthew: "But try to see it from where I was at — the panic, the incredible stress that stays with you 24 hours-a-day. You're living with it. It's inside of you, so you can make some sense out of it. I've talked to other cancer patients and we all seem to ask ourselves the same thing: is it possible to explain all this to kids who have lives of their own and less experience with stress? I thought if I told them I was terrified that I'd die, it would scare them. On the other hand, if I kept everything to myself, I ran the risk of having them think I was angry at *them*.

"I did decide that being honest was the better of these two impossibly hard choices. But my great plan didn't always work out. There were times when I didn't feel like talking to anyone, times when I didn't want anybody around. The most horrible moment of my life was the night Aubrey came into my hospital room to tell me a joke: 'Robber: Your money or your life? Store Keeper: Take my life, I'm saving my money for my old age!' It's a good joke, but I couldn't see the humour. It was as if that part of my brain that knows what funny means had died.''

Aubrey: ''I remember that day, but for me, it was different. I mean my dad is funny. He has a great sense of humour. If he didn't think that joke was a riot, it had to be because he was going through something I couldn't possibly understand. That day I learned to just sit there with him, not saying anything at all. I learned without him even having to tell me that just being there would help him get through another day.''

Generally speaking, if a cancer is discovered early, before cells from the primary tumour have had a chance to break off and spread, it is easier to treat. ''Once a primary tumour has shed some cells, or metastasized,'' says Dr. Hasselback, ''cancer is more difficult to treat because there is more than one site to worry about.''

We can also say that a person who is in good shape — both physically and emotionally — has a better chance of withstanding the terrible months that often go along with cancer treatment.

But there are really no hard and fast rules.

You hear about people whose cancers were *not* diagnosed early, surviving for years and years. You see it with all sorts of different cancers. Sometimes, even the doctors are stumped. Why does this happen? Who knows? Some people attribute the ability to survive against all the odds to the immune system. Other people talk about sheer willpower. For some reason, some cancer patients cope with, and respond to, treatment better than others.

On the other hand, some people whose chances of survival seemed excellent when their treatment was finished, discover a couple of years later that their cancer had spread. At the beginning, it looked as if every last cancer cell had been killed off, that there weren't any cancer cells left alive to spread. In the end, doctors discover that a few cancerous cells, perhaps just one, must have been missed and it is the metastasis, the second tumour, that eventually causes the person to die.

You hear stories, although not many, about cancer patients who have threatened to give up in the middle of their gruelling treatments with radiation, or chemicals. You hear that they have said they just can't take it anymore, that dying in peace would be better than living through what, in their experience, is hell.

It's tempting to say as little as possible about the harshness of radiation therapy and chemotherapy, the two most often used forms of cancer treatment other than surgery. It's very tempting, but unfair.

It's unfair to the person who is in the middle of treatment and needs understanding, respect, and encouragement to go on. And it is unfair to the family. The emotional pain people can go through watching someone suffer is impossible to describe.

Matthew: "Do people really want to know the details of how much, or how little, you feel like throwing up?" For many cancer patients, a side-effect of chemotherapy is nausea and vomiting.

"Do people get bored with you and all your problems? Some days I thought that they did. Even the people who love you are human."

Aubrey: "So he looked a little green at times. That didn't bother me so much, although I must admit I wasn't too thrilled the first time I saw him puke! But to tell the truth, I was happier being there with him than being out with my friends, even during the days when he was so awfully sick."

Matthew: "I didn't want Aubrey to treat me differently, but I *was* different. I needed help with things that a four-year-old could do. There was a period of time when my hands were so weak I couldn't open a jar. I have a picture of myself taken right in the middle of it all. My hair had fallen out from the chemotherapy and I had lost almost 40 pounds. I looked like a plucked chicken, although I couldn't joke about it then!"

Aubrey: "Well he's right about that. He looked like hell. Sometimes I worried that he would die from what they were doing to him. How could so terrible a treatment make anyone well? But looking back, I guess the time did fly by. Before we knew it, he was shovelling the food in again just like normal and complaining that he had to lose a few pounds!"

In the end, when treatment is over, most cancer patients who are cured, or at least in remission and looking forward to some productive months, or years, say the tough time was worth it. Almost every one of the former cancer patients I spoke to talk about each extra day of life as a precious gift — *even better than before*. You hear it so often that you have to wonder . . . . If you were to get cancer and survive, would it teach you something about life that you wouldn't regret having learned?

Matthew: "It does sound corny, but I'm alive and even if it's not forever, each day is a joy. If six years ago someone would have told me I'd be counting days as gifts, I would have laughed. What a dumb thing to say!"

Aubrey: "I think that's a fair way of putting it. He was always fabulous to me, but now there's a kind of sensitivity to him that I don't think was there before . . . ."

Many former cancer patients, not only Matthew, talk a lot about the new ways they have learned to relate to people. This doesn't mean that having cancer is a *good* experience. It's terrible. But sometimes, it takes a rough time to discover just how much you appreciate the people you love.

Matthew: "I've talked about this with Aubrey quite a bit. He and I go fishing together, just the two of us, every July. We both say that we feel lucky in an odd sort of way. We talk about having shared something special — a negative experience, it's true — but one that has touched us both. It's a fantastic feeling to be able to say to one another, 'God, was I ever scared. Was I ever shaking the whole time.' Scared shitless, is the expression Aubrey always loves to use!"

Aubrey: "All my relationships have changed, not just the one with him. The good part is that I can be really close to people. I think I know what friendship really means. But there's a lousy side too, in a way. The kids I go to school with, the ones who haven't been through something like this . . . there's a barrier. It's as if we're living in two different worlds.''

Not everyone I spoke to feels as positive as Matthew and Aubrey, not everyone at all. A few people said that they were never able to muster the kind of inner strength that got Matthew and his family through. They said they didn't know how to share their feelings with their husbands, wives, and children. They hadn't been particularly open with their feelings *before* cancer struck and couldn't suddenly change the way they were used to relating to people.

Some said they just didn't want to ''burden anyone else.'' Others said they just weren't ''the type to talk.'' They are as ''cured'' as Matthew is, at least in the physical sense. But they are still trying to recover the equilibrium that they lost.

In many cases, the family members of these cancer patients said they felt the same way. Their family, which was not close to begin with, fell apart even more. For them, at least for many years, there was little about the experience that was positive, no sharing of fear and of pain. For them, there were just shattered dreams, lost hopes, and the anguish of not knowing what the people you love really think.

It was that way for Jenny, the teenager who said, at the beginning of this book, that knowing more about what cancer is might help her to cope.

Jenny has no brothers or sisters, just a few aunts and uncles and a couple of friends. When I talked to her, two years had passed since her mother Anne had had a breast removed because of breast cancer. Anne's radiation therapy and chemotherapy had been over with for more than a year.

It looks as if Anne is as ''cured'' of breast cancer as Matthew is of leukemia although, strictly speaking, 16 years, not five, must pass after treatment is completed before a doctor will pronounce a former breast cancer patient completely cured. In many ways, life has returned to normal for Jenny and her family. Anne has gone back to work. Jenny is doing better in school. And yet, says Jenny, ''She still looks so different to me.''

Jenny pushes her blonde hair behind her ears when she

speaks. Perhaps it is a nervous reaction, as if, even after two years, she is jumpy in the way that Matthew was those first few weeks.

"It's so confusing," she says, "so difficult to explain. For the first time, I see my mother as a separate person, not just as my mother. She's no longer the one person I can unload my daily troubles onto. She has burdens of her own.

"Maybe this experience could be a good thing, but she won't let me help. It's almost as if she is trying to be a martyr by coping with it by herself. It makes me angry in a way. I want to help. I've wanted to help since the day it all started. But I want her to ask for my help."

Anne: "I can't talk about this to Jenny. I've never been good at sharing these kinds of things; I wasn't brought up that way. I love Jenny, more than you can imagine, and I'm not stupid. I can sense that she's waiting for me to say something. I used to use the excuse that she's just a little girl, that she couldn't handle it, but now I know I'm the one who's afraid."

Jenny: "The other day I said to her, 'Gee mom, if this had been me, I'd really have been scared,' but she just answered, 'Yes, dear.' I got the impression that she was on the verge of saying something, but as usual, she stopped. Maybe she doesn't want to burden me; she's always been like that. On the other hand, maybe she's okay with the whole thing. I really don't know.

"Yesterday I thought I should just tell her how much I love her and how scared I still am and how we should talk, but I chickened out. I always chicken out. She's the one with the experience in life, so she should be the one to start. Great rationalization, eh! She's never had cancer before either.

"I keep worrying if I start talking, there will be a flood of emotions. I'm afraid I'll reach a depth that I've never felt before and I won't be able to rise from it. I feel like I'm standing at the edge of a diving board for the first time with my hands over my head, not wanting to go off. I think of every excuse. It drives me crazy."

Anne: "I don't even talk to Jenny's father about it very much. I know it must sound crazy to all you young people. You're so different than we are, so able to talk about life. It's never been that way for me. Jenny's father Bill and I — we don't use words to tell each other how we feel. It doesn't mean we don't care. But I do wish I could give Jenny what she wants. I think about it all the time. It drives me crazy."

Jenny: "Even my dad doesn't say anything about what's happened. He never gets upset. But I think he feels something. Sometimes, when mom was still in the hospital, I'd come into the house, and he'd be just sitting there, doing nothing, staring into space.

"But whom do I tell all this to? No one I know has ever gone through anything like this. They wouldn't know what I'm talking about. The kids I hang around with would think I'm crazy if I started telling them. And yet, I can't get it out of my mind. I spend a lot of time alone."

Some families are like Matthew's, able to share the pain they are feeling with each other, and it usually helps. The people in families who can talk, and cry, and hold on to each other through the rough days seem to have the easiest of the difficult experiences with cancer.

People in families like Jenny's, where everyone *feels* pain but is too afraid to speak, seem to have a worse time.

Most families, however, are somewhere in between.

Some families start out like Jenny's and slowly, with the help of a psychologist, psychiatrist, social worker, family doctor, member of the clergy, or good friend learn how to share their emotions. Sometimes, it is the parents who realize that they would all do better to talk. Other times, it's the kids themselves who muster the courage to make it happen.

In some communities, schools and community centres have developed programs to help. The Canadian Cancer Society has one such program called "Coping with Cancer" which anyone — adult or teenager — can join. Some members have cancer, or have had it; others love someone who does. Matthew, for example, leads a group that meets twice a month. "Some people turn to professionals for help and it works for them," he says, "but many people who come to our group say that talking to others who've been there is also a tremendous help."

Anyone can find out about "Coping with Cancer" by calling a local branch of the Canadian Cancer Society.

But knowing what may happen and what to expect, also puts

people in a better position to cope with cancer. When all is said and done, when the news that cancer has struck begins to feel real, rather than like a bad dream, knowledge also helps people get through. Once they know the facts about cancer treatment, most people find that they are in a better position to use the rest of their energy to give, or receive, emotional support.

The Diagnosis of Cancer

To make a firm diagnosis of cancer, cells from a person's body must be examined by a doctor called a pathologist whose specialty is identifying disease. There are signs and symptoms that make doctors suspect that a patient has cancer, and they will start looking for cancerous cells. But a final diagnosis cannot be made until cells are actually studied in a lab, under a microscope, and proven to be cancerous.

Most of the time, there is a tumour — which may or may not be cancerous — whose cells can be examined. The exception is leukemia, the type of cancer which Matthew had. Because leukemia is spread throughout a system, the bloodstream, there

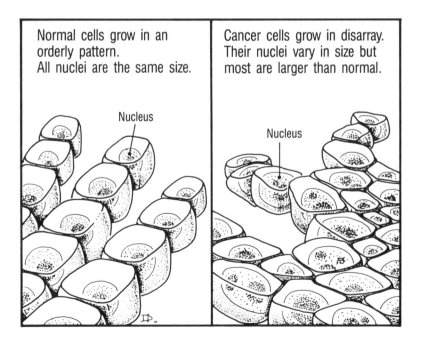

Normal cells grow in an orderly pattern. All nuclei are the same size.

Cancer cells grow in disarray. Their nuclei vary in size but most are larger than normal.

Nucleus

Nucleus

is no actual tumour. Instead, the bone marrow, where the diseased blood cells are produced, must be examined for cancerous cells.

Most tumours do not turn out to be cancerous. Eight out of 10 breast tumours, for example, are "benign" or noncancerous. Benign tumours are removed, and that is the end of it. They do not metastasize, or spread, like cancerous or "malignant" tumours. They can be dangerous, but only because they sometimes grow, getting in the way of other vital organs and tissue.

Getting a sample of cells to study is called "taking a biopsy." Sometimes, the whole tumour is removed, and this is called an "excisional" biopsy. Other times, when only a section of the tumour is cut away, it is called an "incisional" biopsy. In the case of leukemia, a bit of bone marrow is "aspirated", or sucked up, with a long thin needle. The pathologist uses a microscope, as well as blood tests, to determine if the marrow is producing cancerous, or normal, white blood cells.

Sometimes, as was the case with Anne, doctors start looking for a cancer tumour because something unusual turns up during a routine checkup.

Other times, the patient is the one who becomes suspicious. Like Matthew, he or she notices one of the 10 basic signs that the Canadian Cancer Society warns people to watch out for. They are:

1. A sore that does not heal.
2. A change in a mole or wart.
3. The sudden appearance of a lump or a bump.
4. A cough that continues to worsen for several weeks, or blood in the sputum.
5. Vaginal discharge or bleeding other than during a menstrual period.
6. A *change* in one's bowel habits: constipation, or diarrhea.
7. Blood in the urine.
8. Persistent pain.
9. Persistent fever.
10. Unexplainable weakness, or weight loss, or exhaustion over a period of time.

It is particularly sad when a person notices one of these signs or symptoms but, out of fear perhaps, delays going for a medical checkup. Too many doctors can tell stories of cancer patients who could have been helped, if only the treatment had been started earlier.

Sometimes, a tumour is relatively easy to find. Other times, it is more difficult to locate.

When a tumour is accessible, taking a biopsy is usually easy. For instance, it is almost always a simple procedure to obtain a sample of cells from a suspicious-looking tumour on the cervix (the entrance to the womb), and taking a biopsy from a suspicious-looking skin tumour is usually easy as well. These can generally be performed right in a doctor's office with only a local anaesthetic.

Having a bit of bone marrow aspirated requires a brief stay in a hospital. The procedure is usually painful, but only for a moment. The skin is first anaesthetized, then a long syringe, or needle, is inserted into the marrow of a bone, usually a hip bone, but sometimes a breast bone. Finally, a small amount of the marrow is sucked up, the entire procedure taking only a few minutes.

In Anne's case, the cancerous breast was easy to locate, but more difficult to biopsy. Her doctor, who was performing a routine checkup, could feel the lump which was growing in one of Anne's breasts. But to get a sample of cells, Anne had to have a general anaesthetic and then a minor surgical procedure. While the pathologist in the lab determined that the tumour was actually cancerous, Anne remained under general anaesthesia, and then, during the same operation, the cancerous breast was "ressected" or removed.

Other times, when a tumour is growing in an organ such as the kidney, pancreas, or liver (which are all located deep within the body) a major surgical procedure must be performed to obtain cells for a biopsy.

But most of the time, surgery is not required. Because of recent advances in diagnostic methods, tumours in many organs can be located and biopsied in one simple procedure called "endoscopy." An endoscope is a long, thin, instrument made of flexible fibres called fibre optics which can actually transmit light. There is also a pair of tiny "scissors" at the end of most endoscopes. Endoscopes can be inserted into many organs of the body: the lungs, stomach, colon, uterus, and bladder are some of the organs which are now accessible through endoscopy.

In fact, although it is never done, a doctor could technically insert one endoscope through the mouth into the stomach and another through the rectum into the intestinal tract and they could meet in the middle!

Once an endoscope is inside an organ, the doctor turns on the light and looks around for a tumour. If one is visible, the trigger is pressed and snip! A piece of tissue is snared, carefully withdrawn, and sent to the lab for examination.

There are many types of endoscopes. Colonoscopes, for example, are used to examine the entire length of the colon; gastroscopes are used to examine the stomach; cystoscopes are used to examine the bladder.

Many of the cancer patients I spoke to had been terrified of having a biopsy taken with an endoscope. They had heard stories about how painful it was to get a sample of lung, stomach, or colon tissue by this method. Ten years ago, this was true. The endoscopes that were used were not flexible and it was often painful to insert the instrument, especially if the tumour was deep within the organ. This is no longer the case. Today, endoscopy is sometimes uncomfortable, but rarely painful.

To get a biopsy from a lung tumour, for example, a type of endoscope called a bronchoscope is used. The doctor sprays an anaesthetic into the throat and then gently inserts the flexible tube down the throat right into a bronchus, or airway, to a lung. Once the instrument is in place, the light goes on, and the tissue that lines the airway is examined. Most lung tumours develop in the airway to a lung.

If there is a tumour, the doctor will remove a sample of tissue and place a tiny piece between two pieces of glass for protection, and send it to the lab. There, the pathologist will examine the cells and make the decision: are the cells cancerous? And, if they are, exactly what kind of cancer is it?

When cancer is being diagnosed, other tests are usually performed as well. Some of them can determine whether or not the first tumour has spread.

The blood, for example, is chemically tested to see if it contains the normal amount of white blood cells, red blood cells, enzymes, proteins, and minerals.

For most kinds of cancer, the X-ray is an important test. Only a few years ago, normal X-rays — a beam of X-rays and film much like the kind you use in your camera — were usually used. Over the past decade, however, the whole field of X-ray technology has been changing.

In some hospitals, "CT Scanners" (sometimes called CAT Scanners, which stands for Computer Aided Tomography) are used to take pictures of small areas deep within the body. The pictures — paper-thin "slices" of organs — that CT Scanners provide are incredible. Already, CT Scanners are taking the place of many of the more complicated and uncomfortable tests.

Another new way of getting pictures similar to those provided by CT Scanners is through "NMR," nuclear magnetic resonance. These pictures can be taken without exposing the patient to any radiation at all!

Sometimes, just before an X-ray is taken, the patient is given an injection of a type of dye which acts as a contrast, making whatever the doctor is looking for stand out better. These dyes are harmless and painless. They are sometimes used when ordinary X-rays are taken, and before some CT Scans.

"Bone scanners" work on the principle that tumour cells react differently than normal cells to "radioactive isotopes" which can be injected into the blood. During a bone scan, tumour cells — which divide more quickly than normal cells — show up as "hot spots." This is a fast, completely painless method of pinpointing a tumour in a bone that is sometimes as small as a centimeter in diameter. Once the exact location of a tumour is known, it is much easier to obtain a biopsy to determine if it is malignant or benign.

If there is fluid in the chest cavity, the abdomen, or in a joint, some of it will be extracted and examined for cancerous cells. First, a local anaesthetic is injected, then a long, but extremely thin needle is inserted. A bit of fluid is then suctioned out with little discomfort.

Sometimes, some of the fluid in the spinal canal is examined as well. A "spinal tap" used to be a scary and uncomfortable experience. But these days, with better equipment and a tiny needle to freeze the area before the larger one is inserted, a pinprick is all that most people feel.

Once the question, "Is it cancer?" has been affirmed by the pathologist, the next step will be to decide exactly what kind of cancer it is, how far it has progressed, and what the treatment should be.

The Terms That Are Used

Cancer can develop in almost all of the body's organs. The heart, whose cells do not reproduce after maturity, is a notable exception.

Doctors divide the many different types of cancer into five main groups: carcinomas, leukemias, lymphomas, myelomas, and sarcomas.

Carcinomas, such as lung cancer, breast cancer, cancer of the colon, rectum, cervix, and stomach are by far the most common.

Carcinomas begin in "epithelial" cells. These are the cells which line the inside and outside surfaces of the different organs of the body.

Cancerous tumours of the cervix, for example, begin in the epithelial cells that line the organ's *external* surface; cancerous tumours of the colon, on the other hand, begin in the epithelial cells which line the *internal* surface of that organ.

Leukemias are cancers of various types of "leukocytes," or white blood cells that are produced in the bone marrow.

Lymphomas are cancers of the "lymphocytes", the white blood cells of the lymphatic system.

Myelomas are cancers of particular white blood cells called plasma cells which start off as B lymphocytes and then move into the lymphatic system where they mature further into plasma cells. Plasma cells are stored in bone marrow.

Sarcomas are cancers of "mesodermal" cells: bone, muscle, cartilage, tendon, and ligament cells which form supportive and connective tissues.

Cancers which begin in the brain are so different from any other type of cancer that they are usually discussed separately.

Cancer cells usually go through a stage — called precancer — during which they look abnormal, but not so abnormal that pathologists consider them cancerous. Sometimes, precancerous cells can be detected, but not because they exhibit symptoms. They are detected through mass screening programs, such as the Pap test, which are now performed in the hope of detecting precancerous cells of the cervix. The cells of the cervix, for example, go through precancerous changes, called dysplasia, before cancer actually occurs. Precancerous changes may reverse themselves with no treatment at all. And even when they don't, they are relatively easy to cure.

If a precancerous cell does change into a cancer cell, it will usually develop on the surface of the organ. At that point, it is called an ''in situ,'' or early cancer. Like precancerous conditions, early cancers are usually relatively easy to treat successfully.

However, as it begins to spread, a cancer will invade the tissue on which it is growing. At this point, it is referred to as an ''invasive cancer.'' But as long as the cells remain in a single mass — that is, as long as no cells have metastasized from the primary tumour — the cancer is said to be ''localized.''

Then metastasis begins. First, a few cells break off from the primary tumour and travel through the blood vessels or the lymphatic channels to other parts of the body.

Sometimes, the cells that move into the lymphatic system get trapped for a while in the bean-shaped lymph nodes that are found at different points along this system. Usually, it is the first few shed cells that get trapped by a lymph node, and more often than not, the nodes are those that are nearby — that is, *in the region of* the original tumour. When this happens, the spreading process is slowed down for a while, and the cancer is labelled ''invasive cancer with regional involvement.'' This is what Anne's breast cancer was labelled.

If there is no treatment, or the treatment is unsuccessful, cancer cells will almost always spread to more distant parts of the body where they will grow into ''secondary tumours.'' This is ''advanced'' cancer. There are always exceptions, but generally speaking, it is almost impossible to cure cancer once it has reached the advanced stage. Most people with advanced cancer die within five years.

One of the reasons that the death rate from cancer is as high as it is, is because it is usually not detected until it has reached at least the invasive, and often, the advanced stage. This is often nobody's fault. It's just that there are frequently no symptoms — no pain, and nothing suspicious to notice — while cancer is still at an early stage. The only thing that doctors and researchers can stress is this: if someone notices anything suspicious, any of the symptoms listed on page 60, they should get checked by a doctor right away. Cancer generally becomes deadly only when it has invaded an organ, or when it has spread, and often it can be detected before this occurs.

The name doctors give to a particular type of cancer depends on where it begins. If a cancer tumour begins in a breast, for example, it is always called breast cancer. It is still called breast cancer if it spreads to another part of the body, say the lungs. Even if the breast has been removed, and a new tumour develops in a lung from a shed breast tumour cell many years down the road, it would still be referred to as breast cancer. Technically, doctors would call it a ''breast cancer which has metastasized to the lung.'' The breast tumour would have been the primary tumour and the lung tumour would be a secondary tumour.

This makes sense when you recall that the cancer cells which have metastasized to the lung to form a secondary tumour, will still be *breast* cells, not lung cells.

Cancer Treatment

There are basically three main types of cancer treatment: surgery, radiation therapy, and chemotherapy. Often, a combination of two of these three treatments is used. And sometimes, as was the case with the treatment for Anne's breast cancer, all three are used.

Researchers are also constantly seeking ways of improving these treatments. New forms of radiation have been developed. New drugs, and better ways of using the established formulae for existing drugs, are always being found. Completely new methods are being developed as well. Immunotherapy, for example, which tries to stimulate the body's own immune system, is one. How long it will take before these new treatments are available to all cancer patients is impossible to say, but cancer research has never looked as promising as it does today.

Surgery

Many things are taken into account before surgery is chosen as a treatment for cancer. First of all, there must be a tumour. The entire blood stream, for example, can't be surgically removed, and so surgery for leukemia is out of the question. Second of all, the tumour must be able to be reached, and it must be in an organ that can be "ressected," or removed, without causing death. A breast tumour, like the one Anne had, can be ressected; a breast is not essential to life. A liver tumour, on the other hand, cannot be removed. By the time a cancerous liver tumour is detected, it has usually invaded the entire organ. For surgery to be successful, the liver would have to be removed and a person can't survive without a liver.

If the conditions are favourable and the patient is not too old or too ill to withstand surgery, the tumour usually will be removed. Working ever so gently to avoid knocking off any cells which could spread, the surgeon will cut away all the cancer tissue that can be seen, as well as a margin of surrounding normal tissue.

Normal tissue is removed as a preventive measure, mostly because cancer tumours don't grow in tight lumps. Like a patch of crab grass growing in a lawn, cancer tumours have root-like projections which branch off from the main body. Remember the crab? It is important that the surgeon remove enough tissue for a safety margin. If any cells were to be left behind — technically, if one cancer cell was left behind — a new tumour could possibly grow.

Surgery has certainly changed over the past couple of decades. There are better "antibiotics" — the drugs used to control infection — and better anaesthetics that don't leave patients feeling quite so wiped out.

Surgeons have also learned to perform cancer operations in a much more delicate way. Breast surgery, for example, has changed significantly. In the past, the tumour, the rest of the breast, the muscle underneath the breast, and all the glands nearby — the lymph nodes — were all removed. Today, disfiguring "radical mastectomies" are not performed nearly as often.

Anne had a breast and a number of lymph nodes removed. In her case, enough tissue was able to be saved so that a "prosthesis," or breast mold, could be easily fitted. Anyone who is unaware that Anne has had a mastectomy would certainly not realize it from looking at her, "even when I am wearing a low-cut evening gown!" she has to admit.

"Radical surgery for breast cancer," says Dr. Hasselback, "is performed less than half the time. Instead, if a surgeon feels that any cancer cells have already metastasized from the main tumour, either radiation therapy, or chemotherapy, or both, will be used to 'mop them up'."

Radiation Therapy

Since radiation affects any cell that is in the middle of dividing, it ought to affect more cancer cells than normal cells. Why? Because cancer cells, if you recall, divide far more frequently than normal cells. This was the reasoning behind the development of radiation therapy for the treatment of cancer, and the reason why it is still used today.

Radiation doesn't exactly *kill* cancer cells. Rather, it damages the DNA in the nucleus of these cells, and when its DNA is damaged, a cell cannot divide. When cancer cells can no longer divide, they die. Therefore, instead of growing larger, a cancerous tumour that is hit with radiation will shrink.

As with surgery, radiation therapy has certain limitations. For one thing, it can only be used on an organ that stays fixed. Most of us don't think about it very much, but the colon, for example, is an organ that keeps moving around. Waving throughout the abdomen as it goes about its business of digesting food and moving waste, the colon is like a moving target. A radiology oncologist can't aim radiation at a target that moves, and so cannot use it for cancer of the colon.

Some organs can tolerate more radiation than others. The cells of the pancreas, for example, can handle much more radiation than can the cells of the kidneys. The kidneys are located in front of the pancreas, however, and so, to shrink a cancer tumour of the pancreas, a radiologist would have to use more radiation than the cells of the kidney can withstand. That's one reason why radiation cannot be used to shrink a tumour of the pancreas.

Radiation therapy works best on a fixed tumour, or group of tumours, spread over a large accessible area. Hodgkin's disease, a lymphoma in which a group of lymph nodes are involved, is an example of a type of cancer for which radiation therapy works especially well.

Radiation therapy has changed significantly over the years. In the 1920s and 30s, radiation therapy was all but useless for any type of cancer other than skin cancer. It's not that it didn't work: it did. But regular X-rays were not very strong and in order to deliver enough radiation to shrink a tumour deep within the body, so much had to be used, that normal tissue was extensively damaged. The skin was burned, and all the tissue between the skin and the tumour was damaged as well. For that reason, radiation had to be confined to tumours growing on the skin.

Then, in 1956, cobalt radiation was discovered. Cobalt is a metal that can be made radio-active and the rays it delivers are much stronger than regular X-rays. Using cobalt machines, radiologists were able to deliver ''megavoltage'' radiation to tumours deep within the body without damaging organs in between.

Sometimes, tumours can be completely destroyed by radiation and the patient can be cured with no other treatment. Other times, a tumour can be shrunk sufficiently so that curative surgery becomes possible. And in still other cases, radiation is used in conjunction with chemotherapy.

Radiation is now being used in other ways as well. Sometimes, ''needles'' made out of radio-active material are inserted directly into a tumour, and then removed after the treatment is finished. This is a fabulous advance for tumours of the head or neck which, if treated surgically, would leave very severe scars.

The advances in radiation therapy have also been exciting for patients with certain other specific kinds of tumours. A rare type of eye cancer called retinoblastoma which strikes young children, can now often be cured with radiation therapy. Because surgery can be avoided, these children do not lose the use of an eye.

The same type of advance has been made using radiation therapy for cancer of the larynx, or voice box. In the days when this type of cancer could only be treated by surgery, the entire larynx had to be removed and patients lost their ability to speak. With radiation therapy, there is no need for surgery and many former cancer of the larynx patients are living totally normal lives.

Recently, doctors have been successful at radiating the entire body for certain types of leukemia and lymphoma.

Even when a cancer has progressed too far for a cure to be possible, radiation can sometimes be used. Some types of tumours can be shrunk enough to prolong the patient's life for several years. For advanced cancers, radiation can sometimes be used to relieve pain when a tumour presses on a bone, or other tissue.

Although radiation therapy has advanced by leaps and bounds, it is still difficult for cancer patients to cope with in certain ways.

People who receive radiation therapy to their heads still lose their hair just as they did several decades ago. The cells which attach the hair to the head — called hair follicles — divide much more quickly than most normal cells. Because of this, the DNA in these cells is destroyed by radiation in the same way as cancer cells' DNA. Without DNA, the hair cells cannot reproduce, and the hair falls out.

While hair loss is emotionally upsetting, it is not a terrible price to pay in exchange for life. For one thing, hair grows back as soon as treatment is finished. But the other side effects of radiation therapy are worse.

The cells that line the stomach and intestines are also fast-dividing and so, radiation to the abdomen causes severe nausea, vomiting, and diarrhea.

The white blood cells which protect the body from infection have an extremely short life span — only eight hours, in fact. During radiation therapy, their DNA is destroyed and they are unable to divide to replace cells that have died of old age. For this reason, people undergoing radiation therapy have too few white blood cells to perform the important job of fighting off infection. Fortunately, researchers have developed better antibiotics to help combat infection.

As well, the numbers of platelets which protect against bleeding often get low and people bruise easily and find that injuries don't heal.

These side effects last only as long as the radiation treatments continue, and they are not nearly as severe as they once were.

Radiation Therapy — New Research
The first studies on humans using a variation of radiation therapy — pion beam therapy — are beginning to show some extraordinary results for tumours located deep within the body. This is particularly exciting since conventional cobalt therapy has been almost useless for cancers of the brain, pancreas, and bladder.

Pions are the subatomic, glue-like particles that hold together the neutrons, protons, and electrons contained in the nuclei of all cells. Now, pions can be extracted by machines called cyclotrons. When the Los Alamos, New Mexico, centre (where the atomic bomb was developed) was closed a few years ago, only two centres which worked with pions were left — one in Switzerland, the other in Canada. Dr. Gabriel Lam, a research biophysicist at the B.C. Cancer Research Centre in Vancouver, B.C., has been working with pions on Canada's $55 million cyclotron machine for 10 years.

''Cyclotrons extract pions by breaking apart the neutrons, protons, and electrons in cells' nuclei, which causes them to release a pion,'' he explains. But it wasn't until the 1970s that enough pions were able to be extracted to make experiments on cancer tumours possible.

Pions are delivered to cancer tumours by an electromagnetic beam. When the pions hit the cancer cells, they release energy — like a depth charge — and the cancer cells die. Pion beams do very little damage to the tissue that they pass through on their way to cancer tumours and they are also strong enough to reach tumours that are too deep for cobalt radiation.

Unfortunately, it will still be years before pion beam radiation therapy is available to most cancer patients. One of the biggest obstacles in getting this type of therapy into use is the price. The type of cyclotrons required by hospitals to extract pions don't cost $55 million, but they do cost between five and 10 million dollars each!

A further variation on radiation therapy which Dr. Lam is beginning to investigate is neutron beam therapy. Neutrons are also subatomic particles, and they too can be extracted from the nucleus of cells with a cyclotron machine. Whether or not they too will prove useful in cancer treatment remains to be seen. Dr. Lam believes that they will be effective for many more types of cancer than are pion beams, which are only useful for deep tumours. The other advantage to neutron beam radiation therapy is that the type of cyclotron machine required to produce neutrons costs less — approximately $2.5 million.

Chemotherapy

The most exciting advances in cancer treatment have been made with chemotherapy. Over the years, cancer-killing chemicals have saved, or at least extended, the lives of tens of thousands of cancer patients around the world.

Chemotherapy began during World War II when a doctor from the University of Chicago, Charles Huggins, filled a syringe with the female hormone estrogen, and injected it into the bloodstream of a man with cancer of the prostate. Within a few weeks, the growth of the man's tumour slowed down and, for the first time in history, a drug had been used effectively in the battle against cancer.

The beauty of treating cancer with chemicals is that drugs can travel throughout the bloodstream. With surgery, only the tumour itself can be removed. With radiation, except in a few circumstances when it is used on the whole body, the beam can only be aimed at one specific place. That's fine if the cancer tumour has not spread. But too often, at least a few cells have already metastasized from the main tumour by the time surgery or radiation therapy is performed. These shed cells may have already formed a ''micro-metastasis,'' a tiny secondary tumour, some distance away. A long time may pass, years sometimes, before a micro-metastasis actually grows into a secondary tumour that is large enough to be detected. But because chemotherapy travels throughout the body via the bloodstream, many cancer patients who receive this kind of treatment are now being cured.

In the late 1940s, a group of researchers at Yale University in Connecticut began to expand on Dr. Huggins' experiments by making use of a chance disaster. During World War II, the

U.S. was trying to develop chemicals for use in warfare when some mustard gas with which they were experimenting, exploded. The Yale scientists read that the people killed in the explosion had died because the gas had damaged their white blood cells.

The Yale researchers suggested that they could use a similar chemical to fight lymphoma, cancer of the lymph system, since it's so good at killing off white blood cells. It made sense since the problem with lymphoma patients is that they have too many white blood cells.

They tried nitrogen mustard, a chemical related to mustard gas, on a patient with cancer of the lymphatic system. Sure enough, the cancerous white blood cells disappeared, although only for a short time. Today, more than 30 years later, the drug is still used, although more skillfully, to treat Hodgkin's disease, a specific type of lymphoma.

At about the same time, another major advance using chemicals was made. This time, Dr. Sidney Farber, the doctor for whom the world-famous Sidney Farber Cancer Institute in Boston is named, was responsible. He realized that the cancer cells of children with leukemia grew faster if the children were given large amounts of a certain vitamin B.

If a drug could be made to *interfere* with the body's use of this vitamin, Dr. Farber speculated, it might inhibit the cancer cells as well.

In his lab, Dr. Farber came up with a drug called "aminopterin." For 10 out of the 16 dying children he first tried it on, aminopterin brought successful, although temporary, results.

Because of pioneers like these, a huge program to develop chemotherapy was started in the 1950s in the United States. It began with five million dollars that the American Congress gave to the NCI, the National Cancer Institute of the United States, the American equivalent of the NCIC, National Cancer Institute of Canada, which funds cancer research in Canada. Since the program was started, approximately 40 anti-cancer drugs have been discovered or created.

Chemotherapy is being used increasingly for cancers like leukemia which cannot be treated by surgery. And doctors are achieving some excellent results, especially with children. In the beginning, only one drug was generally tried for one kind of cancer. Now, a combination of drugs is usually used.

Some of these drugs stop cancer cells from making the DNA they need in order to begin the first stage of cell division. Others work by paralyzing the cancer cells while they are in the middle of dividing. And still others, like methotrexate which was an advancement on Dr. Farber's aminopterin, trick cancer cells by masquerading as vitamins.

Methotrexate is like the Trojan horse which looked like a horse but, indeed, was not. To the cancer cell, methotrexate *looks* like vitamin B, but when the cancer cell "eats" this vitamin, it soon finds that it has taken in something which it cannot digest. Cancer cells literally choke on cancer drugs like methotrexate.

Today, chemotherapy is often used in conjunction with surgery, or radiation therapy, and sometimes with both. In many cases, chemotherapy is started almost as soon as a cancer patient comes off the operating table, or a tumour has been shrunk by radiation.

Why wait to see if a metastasis shows up, when chemotherapy can be used right away? The hope is that if a few shed cells from the primary tumour have been missed, they will be killed by chemotherapy *before* they have a chance to grow into secondary tumours. The name of this type of chemotherapy treatment is called "adjuvant chemotherapy." When it is successful, a second tumour never develops. Over the past few years, adjuvant chemotherapy has been used for breast cancer patients like Anne. It is too soon to know for sure, but oncologists like Dr. Hasselback believe that more and more successes are going to be seen because of it.

That is the beauty of chemotherapy, but there is an ugly side to it as well. Almost all of the drugs that are used to fight cancer are poisonous. They cause worse side effects than radiation therapy or surgery.

When having radiation therapy to their heads, patients' hair falls out. All chemotherapy drugs, however, travel throughout the bloodstream. Almost all of the drugs affect the blood vessels of the scalp where the hair follicle cells are located. Therefore, *most* chemotherapy patients lose their hair. As with radiation therapy, hair grows back when the chemotherapy is over, but hair loss is not the worst side effect of this type of treatment.

Nausea and vomiting are often a side effect of the chemicals that are used. As well, the DNA of the fast-dividing cells that line the mouth and the throat is damaged; for this reason some patients lose their sense of taste and the ability to swallow without discomfort.

Matthew remembers those first weeks of intensive chemotherapy: "I was on a very heavy dose of several drugs for five days; they must have mixed up that devil concoction in a blender! Then they let me off for a few weeks to recover. At the end of those three weeks, they did another bone marrow test to see if I was in 'remission', if all the cancer cells appeared to have been killed. The drugs had worked; I *was* in remission. But God, during those first five days there were times when I'd be throwing up every 20 minutes. Some nights I didn't believe I had the courage to go on."

Aubrey: "You'd look at him in the morning and you'd think he'd been through a war. But once those first five days were over, it wasn't quite as bad. You could see his strength coming back, little by little."

One of the greatest problems for people who are undergoing chemotherapy is weight loss. Food is not appealing when you can't taste it, and when you feel like throwing up. Some people find that eating a large number of small meals each day, rather than three large ones, is helpful. Other people try to keep their weight up by snacking on tasty, high calorie treats, like milk shakes. Most people try to avoid fatty foods which are particularly hard to digest. An entire booklet, advising people on how to cope with weight loss and nutrition while on chemotherapy, has been published by the Canadian Cancer Society.

Matthew: "During those first five days I ate nothing. Nothing! Then, I started on a few things. Potato chips, I loved potato chips. Crazy, eh? Most cancer patients find them too rich, too hard to digest. But that was one of the first things I could eat when my five-day journey was over."

Aubrey: "I brought him his first bag. Onion-flavoured! It was funny to watch him. Before that he'd sort of push his food around, trying to hide things under pieces of lettuce so we'd think he was eating. I used to do that when mom cooked liver. But you should have seen him with those chips. Boy, what a pig!''

Some cancer patients have found that smoking marijuana — that's right, pot — helps with the nauseating side effects of chemotherapy. For years, many people, except the police who made a few arrests, did not take the idea of pot for cancer patients very seriously. Then, a number of doctors told their patients that they would go to court on their behalf if they were arrested for smoking marijuana, and more people began to take the risk.

Eventually, a pharmaceutical company created a marijuana-like pill called Nabalone which is synthesized from the part of the marijuana plant that seems to calm people. Some people insist that it has been a lifesaver. Others say Nabalone does nothing much for them at all. A few people say that it has its own side effects, such as making time seem as if it is passing more slowly. These people usually say that Nabalone makes them feel worse.

Matthew: ''They gave me Nabalone during those first five days. At first I liked it. I felt, you know, high.''

Aubrey: ''You should have seen him. One time I walked in and he was in the bathtub singing. I mean, talk about role reversals. My father stoned out of his tree.''

Matthew: ''A couple of days later, the effects sort of wore off. I know other people for whom Nabalone has worked better. I just became more aware of my stress.''

Chemotherapy, like radiation therapy, also affects the normal blood cells which, like cancer cells, divide frequently. Patients become extremely tired and susceptible to infections. Sometimes, their gums bleed, and they bruise more easily than usual.

What's worse is that for the past few years, oncologists have been giving patients stronger doses of drugs for longer periods of time in the hope of killing every last cancer cell that may have escaped surgery or radiation therapy.

Each phase of chemotherapy is planned to fit the patient's exact needs. How a patient reacts to the drugs, of course, is also taken into account. Generally, a course of therapy is planned in two parts. The first part is designed to kill the bulk of the cancer cells, and is sometimes repeated. The second part is referred to as ''maintenance therapy.''

The first phase is sometimes like Matthew's program. Very strong drugs are administered for a five day period, called a ''course.'' There may be several courses over a number of months. This phase is designed to put the patient into remission and is the roughest part. Matthew was lucky. He went into remission after the first five-day course. His two additional courses, one in February, the next in March, were given for added protection, in case some cancer cells had been missed during the first course.

Other cancer patients get the first phase once a week for a month, either all at once, or over a period of a couple of days. Some are on drugs steadily for a month, getting one type one week, and another type the next. How a patient reacts to treatment depends on what drugs are used and the individual's ability to cope with them, and stress.

Maintenance therapy can sometimes last as long as a couple of years. The drugs used during this second phase are rarely as strong as during the first phase. Most cancer patients can live normal lives during the second phase of chemotherapy.

Some maintenance therapy patients come into the hospital for a few days each month, and take pills or injections at home in between. The luckiest are able to take all the drugs they need in tablet form. Some people do suffer mild side effects, but the emotional stress of wondering if the chemicals will keep the cancer in remission is usually far worse than any physical discomfort they have.

Matthew: ''That second part, it's true, wasn't so bad. It went on for two years. I felt awful at times — nauseated and tired. But the fear was far worse than the physical symptoms. It was like a humming in the background, a radio that was never quite turned off. Secretly, I called it my background Muzak, and every time I had to go in for another blood test to ensure that I was still in remission, the volume of my Muzak went up. Diana and I tried not to lay too much of that on the kids. But I can remember buying Sol a little two-wheeler with training wheels at the end of that first year. At that point, I wasn't convinced that I'd see him ride that bike by himself. I don't worry about it all that much anymore."

Aubrey: "He thinks we didn't know. But after a while, we got to know his schedule. Four days before he went in for a blood test, he'd get a bit cranky. The day before, he was a wreck. But it didn't last. I don't think I worry about it all that often anymore."

Oncologists hope that the side effects of these stronger, and longer-lasting courses of treatment, will be balanced on the positive side by better results. But for many of the newer drug combinations, the results are still unknown. "It takes years sometimes," says Dr. Hasselback, "to be certain that a metastasis is not going to show up. Breast cancer patients are not considered totally cured for approximately 16 years after treatment. Leukemia patients must wait five years for a completely clean bill of health. Lymphoma patients must wait eight years, and for most types of carcinoma, five years after treatment are necessary. Part of the anguish is waiting to see."

Matthew: "I guess now it's mostly Christmas and birthdays that make me a little edgy. I get a sort of bitter-sweet feeling. It means much more to me to be here for another year. But you know, rare as it is, leukemia patients off treatment for six years have gone out of remission before."

Aubrey: "I guess it crosses all of our minds at Christmas. Birthdays too, especially his. But we'll make it. I know someone who has been cured of leukemia for 15 years. I think it helps that we sometimes still talk about it. The fact that we could always talk about it when we needed to, is what really got us through."

Immunotherapy

Cancer researchers called "immunologists" are working to learn more about the possibilities of the latest development in cancer treatment to date: immunotherapy. Until a few years ago, "immunology" sparked very little interest among the public. Then someone got wind of the research being done with a drug called Interferon and, like wildfire spreading, the news hit the stands.

Other exciting areas of immunology are being studied as well: bone marrow transplantation, monoclonal antibodies, and anti-cancer vaccines are all beginning to yield exciting preliminary results.

INTERFERON

Why did Interferon take the public by storm? Probably because when it was first studied, we were all due for a little uplifting news where cancer research was concerned. Also, the name Interferon seems so positive, so appropriate for a fighter against cancer. When it first became possible to make sufficient quantities of Interferon in the lab for testing purposes, articles with snazzy headlines began to hit the news.

Interferon, said some, was going to become "the new Wonder Drug." It was going to be the new multipurpose chemical that would kick the body's immune system back into gear. What's more, because Interferon is a *natural* chemical, it was going to do all this with no dreadful side effects. And, it was going to do it almost overnight.

It didn't happen quite that way. Investigating a drug like Interferon takes years of painstaking research. Unfortunately, much of the media neglected to mention this minor detail.

So far, Interferon has certainly caused cancer tumours to shrink, but it has not done it any better than many other chemical therapies.

Why not? Part of the reason has to do with the fact that science still lacks a lot of knowledge about the immune system itself.

Does cancer suppress the immune system so much that not even Interferon can get it back into working order? Some studies show that carcinogens like cigarette smoke do mess up the immune system to some degree, but really, scientists don't fully know.

Maybe cancer interferes with the immune system *progressively* as it takes over the body? Interferon has only been used on patients with advanced cancer. Perhaps by that time, it's too late.

Or perhaps, Interferon stimulates only NK cells to work harder than normal? Since NK cells kill only viruses, it could be that Interferon will only be an effective drug for those few types of cancer that are caused by viruses.

When some of these questions are answered, more information about Interferon, and other kinds of immunological treatments, will emerge.

We have to hope that the press will learn to look at these experiments with some restraint. This type of research takes time, as difficult as it is to remain patient when someone we love needs immediate treatment.

In any case, the part about Interferon being natural and free of side effects is true. For this reason — and because we continue to hope — researchers will press ahead with experiments on Interferon and other types of chemicals which might stimulate the immune system to fight against cancer.

VACCINES

Vaccines which would prevent cancer from developing are also being investigated. Experiments with vaccines, on animals, have shown that they can be effective in preventing certain rare types of cancers which are caused by viruses. Perhaps someday, a vaccine will be developed to prevent some types of cancer in humans.

BONE MARROW TRANSPLANTATION

A couple of new areas of immunology do look promising, however. One of them has to do with "bone marrow transplantation".

When a person has leukemia, the bone marrow produces cancerous cells. Certain anti-cancer drugs, like the ones given to Matthew, can sometimes kill these cancerous cells, and the patient goes into remission. At that point, the cells produced by the bone marrow are healthy.

Other times, chemotherapy is not successful. In certain circumstances, usually when the patient is under 40 and in good health, a bone marrow transplant is considered. A donor whose cells have the same HLA markers as the cancer patient's cells must be found to provide marrow for transplantation. If the markers are different, the cancer patient's immune system will perceive the donated marrow as foreign and will not accept it. Often, a brother or a sister of the cancer patient is a suitable donor. Cells from siblings are studied genetically, and if the HLA markers do match, healthy bone marrow is extracted from the donor's hip bone. This marrow is then injected into the cancer patient's bloodstream, much like a transfusion. (If you're interested in more detail, see page 158.) Since the HLA markers are the same, the chances of the cancer patient accepting the transplanted bone marrow are good. If it is accepted, the cancer patient will be able to produce healthy blood cells.

Bone marrow transplantation is, however, a risky procedure. Prior to the transplant, all the cancer patient's bone marrow — and, with luck, all of the cancer cells in it — is destroyed by strong drugs. At that point, no one can say for sure if the transplanted marrow will be accepted, and if it isn't, the patient will die.

In a few centres in the U.S., another type of experiment is being tried on leukemia patients for whom chemotherapy has already been successful. When the patient is in remission, bone marrow is extracted and frozen. The hope is that the leukemia patient will be able to become his or her own donor, *if and when* there is a relapse. Since the bone marrow transplant would be from the patient's own body, the HLA markers would, of course, be the same, and there would be no question of rejection. The one worry would be that a few stray cancer cells may have been frozen in the marrow inadvertently. More research in this area is being done.

MONOCLONAL ANTIBODIES

The other area of immunological research has to do with cells called "monoclonal antibodies." This research is not quite as advanced as the research on bone marrow transplantation, but initial experiments look promising.

If scientists end up with the positive results that the preliminary research is indicating, the dreadful side effects of chemotherapy could be dinosaurs of the past. If scientists are successful in making monoclonal antibodies — and translating them into use on cancer patients which is the current snag — the cancer drugs of the future would act like homing pigeons. Instead of blasting the whole body, cancer cells and normal cells alike, monoclonals will head directly to the cancer cells they are designed to treat. They will not harm a single, solitary, normal cell.

Monoclonal antibodies are made like this: A mouse gets an injection of human cancer cells — the particular kind of cancer the doctor is trying to treat. Because this cancer is from a foreign body (at least as far as the mouse is concerned), the mouse has no trouble recognizing the antigen markers on the surface of the cancer cells. Immediately, the mouse starts making antibodies for the cancer cell antigens.

Remember that as soon as antigen markers sense the presence of a foreign antigen, white blood cells called B lymphocytes start producing antibodies. These antibodies hunt down the antigens for which they were created, marking the cells the antigens are on for destruction.

Next, some of the white blood cells that are producing these particular antibodies are extracted from the mouse. Then, each one is chemically fused to a completely different cancer cell. This double cell is called a ''hybridoma.''

The hybridoma, made up of a cancer cell plus an antibody-producing white blood cell, has two important qualities which you could say it has inherited from its two parents.

From the cancer side of the family, the new cell gets its characteristic of dividing forever. That's one of the qualities of cancer cells discussed in chapter one; cancer cells continue to divide regardless of whether there is a need for new cells.

From the white blood cell side of the family, the hybridoma inherits the ability to produce antibodies that can track down particular antigens — the antigens found on the cells of the type of cancer the doctors are trying to treat, the one injected into the mouse in the first place.

The hybridoma starts dividing, and never stops dividing. It makes exact copies, or clones, of itself, all of which contain the necessary antibody. Next, these antibodies are separated from the hybridomas.

These antibodies go into the bloodstream of the cancer patient and, according to the theory, off they move seeking *only* the cancer cells for which they were created. They ignore any other cells they meet up with along the way.

When they arrive at the cancer cells, they mark them for destruction. T lymphocyte white blood cells come in and finish the job.

So far, monoclonal antibodies have only been tried on a small number of cancer patients. Most of the experiments to date have been done on patients with leukemia, or cancer of the lymphatic system. Since these cancers move throughout the body via one of its systems, it may be easier for monoclonal antibodies to spot the cancer cells for which they were created.

In some research centres, scientists are also experimenting with monoclonal antibodies in another way. They are adding other items to the antibody. In some cases, it is a cancer-killing drug; in other cases, it is radio-active material that allows the monoclonal antibody to be used as a diagnostic tool.

Imagine! A cancer-killing drug attached to an antibody roaming around looking for its proper antigen mate, the cancer cell. Then zap! The antibody attaches itself to the cancer cell and releases its cancer-killing chemical.

When they are used as diagnostic tools, monoclonal antibodies are fused with small amounts of radio-active material instead of cancer-killing drugs. The idea is to be able to find tiny, secondary tumours that are too small to show up on an X-ray. Keep in mind that the earlier they are found, the easier these secondary tumours are to treat.

After the monoclonal antibodies have been fused with the radio-active material, the patient is placed under a scanning machine that can pick up radiation.

When the monoclonals are injected into the bloodstream, they head right for the cancer cells. The machine then follows the radiation in the cells. Within minutes, the scanner picks up the radiation which is, by then, at the cancer site, and the exact location of the tiny tumour is known.

Someday, these kinds of techniques may be available to cancer patients around the world. Someday, because of the research which National Cancer Institutes fund and because of the millions of dollars Cancer Societies raise every year.

And yet, in spite of all these efforts, for many people who have cancer today, these advancements have not come fast enough. In desperation, many people turn to treatments that don't work. They are called ''fringe methods'' by researchers who work in the legitimate field of cancer treatment and research.

Fringe Methods

When you think about Interferon and the premature hopes it created, you begin to see what can happen in the area of cancer treatment. An experiment that should be reported as preliminary research, gets front page billing. Readers infer that the cure for cancer is on the verge of being discovered. In certain newspapers which are more concerned about sales than facts, small bits of progress are even reported as THE CURE.

The legitimate therapies that exist now are not successful for half of the people who get cancer. In a panic to do something, to do anything but give up, many people are tempted to seek out the promises that fringe methods make.

When all else has failed, when the proven treatments don't work anymore, some people will search frantically for anything that *might* help. For them, searching is better than doing nothing. While they are doing something, they can stop thinking about death.

But searching for fringe methods is a different story when a person who might have been cured by legitimate means delays seeking treatment. It is different when someone believes the illogical promises of an instant, and complete cure. For this reason, it's important to understand why fringe methods don't work.

There are no figures for Canada, but every year, Americans spend between two and three *billion dollars* on potions, devices, and ceremonies that promise to cure cancer — any kind of cancer.

Usually, these treatments also promise to accomplish the cure with no pain, and no suffering.

It's easy to see why people want to believe it. Non-poisonous injections can be pretty tempting to people who face chemotherapy.

And while coffee enemas may sound disgusting, they begin to sound a lot less terrible when the alternative is major surgery.

The best known, and most often tried fringe cancer therapy, is "laetrile." Its chemical name is amygdalin. It is also called vitamin B-17, cyto H-3, KH-3, and aprikern. Laetrile is found in apricot pits, peach pits, almonds, and apple seeds.

Those who support laetrile claim that it kills cancer cells

when it releases cyanide, a deadly poison. Laetrile does contain cyanide. In fact, that's part of the problem. Since cyanide is a deadly poison, it has been known to produce worse side effects than the proven anti-cancer chemicals.

Laetrile supporters insist that the cyanide stays locked in the laetrile except when it happens upon cancerous cells. They say this is because cancer cells contain large amounts of a protein called "beta-glucosidase" which releases the cyanide. Normal cells, they say, don't contain very much of this protein, and for this reason, remain unharmed.

Laetrile supporters also say that healthy cells are further protected from the cyanide because they contain "rhodanase" which is supposed to convert cyanide into a harmless substance. Cancer cells supposedly don't contain rhodanase.

The trouble with all these explanations is that scientists have looked for beta-glucosidase in cancer cells and normal cells and have found only traces of it. As well, they have found no more, or less, of it in cancer cells than normal cells.

Scientists have also looked for rhodanase in both cancer cells and normal cells, and have found exactly the same amounts in each.

Nevertheless, because there has been so much controversy, and because so many people have been so interested in laetrile, many separate laetrile experiments have been conducted by scientists over the years. None have shown laetrile to be effective in cancer treatment.

And still the supporters of laetrile carry on. Their claims are very similar to those of others who swear by drugs which scientists have proved useless. Some say the medical community is plotting against them. Others insist that the medical community doesn't really want to see advances made in cancer research because if cancer were cured, it would cost doctors their jobs.

There are other things which supporters of fringe therapies have in common with those who support laetrile. They seem to promote one treatment for all kinds of cancer. To them it makes no difference whatsoever that cancer is really a term for more than 100 different diseases.

They tend not to publish the results of their studies, or the explanations of how the studies were done. Their records —

if there are any records — are usually incomplete. When people insist that they have been miraculously cured of cancer, it is often discovered that no biopsies were ever done. Whether or not the patient actually had cancer to begin with was frequently never proved.

Some people sell handwriting tests — one is called the Kanfer Neuromuscular — that are supposed to detect hidden cancers. Others sell grape cures. There is also the Orgone Energy Device, a gizmo which harnesses energy from the universe to cure cancer.

Groups with high fallutin names like The Cancer Control Society, The Committee for Freedom of Choice in Cancer Therapy, and the National Health Federation support various fringe remedies. It's not so surprising that desperate people believe the stories these organizations tell.

How Legitimate Research Works

Perhaps if people understood more about how legitimate scientists test cancer drugs, the fallacy of the fringe drugs would be more apparent.

In legitimate medical research, the first step in the identification of new chemicals is called screening. Every year, about 150,000 new chemicals are developed worldwide. Since it would be impossible to test them all on humans, they are first tested on mice. If a chemical is found to affect cancer tumour growth, it goes on to the next phase.

In this second step, the chemical is identified. When this has been done, it is tested on other animals: monkeys and dogs.

If the chemical is still found to be safe, it goes on to be tested on humans — in tightly controlled conditions.

There are four stages to the human-testing phase. At the first stage, a drug is only given to a cancer patient whose disease will not respond to any other proven therapy. These patients are informed of the risks involved and the probability of success. Often it's not great. Much of the knowledge gained at this stage has to do with determining the proper dose, rather than curing people.

When a safe dose is found, the second phase begins. Studies

are done to see if the drug affects the growth rate of tumours in humans, and if so, which types of tumours respond.

In the following phases, these drugs are compared with others that are already in use. It is not until the fourth phase that a cancer drug actually makes it into the arsenal of drug therapies.

Since 1955, something like half a million drugs have been tested. Only one out of every 5,000 drugs even reaches the human testing phase. Fewer than one of every 50,000 drugs tested, has ended up on the cancer drug list. So far there are about 40; only 30 are commonly used. It is an extensive and serious testing procedure.

There is another truth to think about in the face of all this. Even after all the years of research, all the time and money, hopes and dreams, for more than half of the people who get cancer, there is no long term cure. *That* is the terrible truth.

One question remains: What do you do when there is nothing left to think about but death?

CHAPTER FIVE

Dying with Cancer

I T CAN happen suddenly, like a brick shattering a pane of glass. You find out that someone you care about has cancer and that they are going to die.

Other times, the realization seeps into consciousness slowly. Someone is in the middle of treatment and things begin to go badly. One day, there is a vague feeling, perhaps because of a comment made by a doctor, or a bit of information in a pamphlet, that clicks. This treatment is not working, and it is not going to work! The doctors are doing all they can, but it is not enough. Perhaps it won't happen tomorrow, or next week, or even next month, but sometime soon this person will be a victim of cancer.

The way our society has looked at death, and the ways in which it has tried to cope with it, have changed slowly over the past 30 years.

In the 1950s, very few people would talk about death, or dying. Most people bore the pain of watching a loved one die without any conversation about how they felt. Perhaps this had to do with the fact that the science of death and dying had not yet been created. I also suspect that people were embarrassed to admit that they sometimes felt angry as well as sad.

In the early 1960s, a few people, mostly psychiatrists, started talking and writing about death.

A few years later, a handful of people in England began building homes, called ''hospices,'' where people who were dying could live comfortably until the end came. Organizations to help people and their families who were trying to cope emotionally with dying and death, were started.

In the 1980s, courses about death and dying were actually developed by professors in universities.

As a result of all this, many people are now trying to understand death as a natural part of the process of life — even when the person who is dying is not old.

Regarding death as natural doesn't mean that people handle it all that much better, or grieve any less. It just means that they believe that talking openly, instead of hiding their feelings, can help them understand this aspect of life a little better. From a period of mourning, and a time of trying to make some sense out of something that is inexplicable, they hope to gather strength to go on with their own lives, cherishing the memory of the person who has died.

Why did people begin to change their attitude towards coping with death and dying? The question is difficult to answer.

One theory is that this new attitude evolved slowly because of natural events. In the 1960s, a few people came to the conclusion that they were better able to cope with death when they didn't hide their feelings. They talked openly about their feelings, wrote books about their experiences, built hospices, and eventually developed courses to teach others what they had discovered. As more people were exposed to the concept of examining their feelings, their experiences also changed. And as more peoples' experiences changed, new books were written and the original philosophy developed even more.

These events were all intertwined. They were both the cause and the effect, and once they gained momentum, there was no way society could turn back.   Historians ask themselves how events get started in the first place. Those who have chosen to investigate the issue of death and dying talk about how our society changed from being largely rural to largely urban. Dr. Dorothy Ley, executive director of The Palliative Care Foundation of Canada, is one of these people.

''In the early part of this century,'' says Dr. Ley, ''the majority of people lived on farms rather than in cities. On farms, dying and death is a more natural part of life.'' Dr. Ley is not trying to suggest that kids who grew up on farms in the 1920s or 30s seeing farm animals die would have felt that the death of a relative was *easy* to accept. But because of their experience, it may have seemed more logical to these kids that people do sometimes die before they are very old.

Today, most teenagers grow up in towns and cities; probably you are one. It may be that you have never before had to think about death in any context. When people have no personal experience with a topic, they tend to turn to intellectual pursuits, like reading books, taking courses, or just talking to others. Some historians feel that this is what began to happen with the subject of death and dying as society became less rural.

When the ''extended'' family began to disappear — when mothers and fathers, and grandparents, and perhaps even a few aunts or uncles no longer lived with all the children under one roof — this theme developed more. When there was no longer someone around to provide comfort in a time of crisis — when a family member was dying, for example — people turned more to society for assistance, and the concept of hospices and palliative care emerged. Perhaps, as people began to believe that society would take care of these needs, they began to feel more relaxed about moving away from their families.

Within a generation or two of all these changes, another important development took place. Around the early 1950s, doctors and their patients began to believe that almost all sickness could be cured.

New machines and new drugs — such as penicillin and the antibiotics that are now commonplace — were turning the practice of medicine into the most exciting science on earth. When people started to see pneumonia patients, for example, being cured for the first time, it gave them another reason to stop accepting death as normal.

Students in medical school in the 1960s didn't have time to think about death and dying; they had enough trouble keeping up with all the new advances in medicine that were being developed to keep people alive.

Many doctors who could suddenly cure people — of polio, of pneumonia, of influenza — didn't want to think any more about those who were dying. To some doctors, a dying patient meant failure, and many of them did not want to be reminded that it was still possible to fail.

A lot of emotional problems followed in the wake of all these changes and today, many people are searching for a balance. Doctors are still trying to learn better methods of treatment. But they are now also trying to remember that people who are dying, and their families, have to cope with how they feel.

The science of caring for people who are dying, called ''palliative care,'' began with a few courageous pioneers.

In England, in the 1960s, a doctor who was knighted for her efforts, Dame Cicely Saunders, raised some money and built a home. She called it St. Christopher's. It was the first hospice.

At St. Christopher's, people who were specially trained took care of men and women who *knew* they were going to die. It was the first ''free-standing'' building whose staff focussed their efforts on palliative care.

The word hospice comes from a Greek word which means ''a resting place during a difficult journey.'' The journey, in this case, is from life to death.

The philosophy of palliative care is to ensure that people are as comfortable and as fulfilled as possible during this difficult journey. It is different from ''curative care,'' for which the hope is always that patients can be cured, or at least have their lives extended for a reasonable length of time.

Places like St. Christopher's are not like ordinary hospitals. There are doctors and nurses who do tests and give drugs. If someone needs a pain-killer — although fewer than half of all cancer patients suffer pain in the last weeks of their lives — the medical staff do everything they can to stop the pain. Instead of trying to cure people, they try to give people comfort.

If a patient needs someone to talk to, a hand to hold, or someone who simply understands the fear that can go along with knowing you are going to die, the hand, the talk, or the understanding will be there. At a hospice, this kind of comfort is available during the day, and in the dark, lonely hours of the night. As long as a person lives, the objective is to make every hour as fine as humanly possible.

But hospices have another goal as well. The philosophy is that when someone who is dying has a family, the members of that family are dying a little too. A son, daughter, wife, husband, mother, father, sister, brother — each person in that family has a need, and each need is recognized as different. There are no rules about visiting hours at places like St. Christopher's; dying is a family affair.

It shocked me when I first heard it put that way — a family affair. Family affairs have always been weddings, and birthdays, and all sorts of happy occasions that I don't normally think of, when I think about death.

In my family, when someone was dying, or had died, we were supposed to act sad. At the same time, we were supposed to pretend that we were strong. Most important of all, we were not supposed to admit that we felt all the different emotions that people usually feel when someone close to them has died.

Is that how it is at a hospice? Well, yes and no is what people who work at places like St. Christopher's would say. They would say yes, because we all feel sad when we must say good-bye forever to someone we love, and sometimes, we do want to pretend that we're strong to make it easier for them. And no, because saying goodbye means remembering some good times, and maybe some bad times, as well. It also sometimes means feeling angry or deserted, even though it's illogical to blame someone who is going to die. It's also sometimes hard to separate emotions like sadness, and anger, and relief.

At the same time as the first hospices were being built in England, Dr. Elizabeth Kubler-Ross, a psychiatrist, was beginning to talk and write about dying and death in the United States.

For the first time, people in America were hearing that the emotions which they were feeling affected others as well. They were finally hearing that it was normal to feel what they thought were negative emotions like anger and relief. Reading Dr. Kubler-Ross's words made them realize that they were not the only ones who felt this way and, perhaps more importantly, that they were not crazy.

To explain to others what happens when people find out that they are going to die, Dr. Kubler-Ross came up with the concept of five ''stages of dying.'' She calls them: denial, anger, bargaining, depression, and acceptance. I never got the impression that Dr. Kubler-Ross meant these five stages to be taken literally — first this happens, then that happens, and that's that. When I read about the stages of dying for the first time many years ago, I took them to be concepts. I saw them as a way of explaining some of the things I had always sensed, but never seen put into words.

Not everyone who is dying goes through Dr. Kubler-Ross's five stages. Some people do not go through any of these stages at all. Others go through them in a different order, or miss one or more stages completely.

I think it has been a tragic error that, in an attempt to make some sense out of something as complex as death, some people looked at what Dr. Kubler-Ross had written and accepted everything she said at face value. Instead of realizing that each person is unique, her ideas were taken as gospel. They believed that five labels alone could be used to conquer emotional pain. The interpretation was too simplistic.

Dr. Kubler-Ross calls the first stage of dying "denial." When people are told that their disease is "terminal," that it cannot be cured and they are going to die, they may say something like, "I don't believe it. It's not true. You read the tests wrong. They got my name wrong. Whatever the screw-up is, this is not happening to me."

Many people who are told, or find out, that they have terminal cancer, are unable to face it, at least for a while.

Sometimes, the members of the dying person's family are also unable to believe the truth. Dr. Kubler-Ross's stages are usually used to describe what people who are dying go through, but their families often go through the same, or similar, stages at the same time, or at a different time. A doctor explains that there is nothing more to be done and yet, it doesn't register. Families pretend that the type of treatment being given is still curative, rather than palliative.

Kassy, one of the many teenagers I spoke to about death and dying, is 16 now. When she was 14, her father Michael, was diagnosed as having lung cancer. Michael died six months after his tumour was detected, shortly after Kassy's fifteenth birthday. A year has passed since then.

''I was away in Calgary when my father found out he had lung cancer and only a few months to live,'' Kassy told me. ''I was visiting my friend Cathy for the summer. Her parents didn't tell me about daddy. He wouldn't let them. He wanted to wait until I came home so he could tell me himself. When he told me he was dying, it was as if a special part of him trusted me enough to say it. 'I won't have you for very much longer, Kassy,' he said.

''We both cried. We held onto each other and as long as my arms were around him, I was sure everything would be okay. I didn't believe it. He was just very sick. He'd get better, I knew that he would.''

Kassy's mom, Florence, had been with Michael when the results of the biopsy revealed a cancerous tumour in Michael's left lung. That was in July, almost a month before Kassy came back from out west.

Florence: ''We didn't believe it at first either. I don't think most people do; it's too much of a shock. But I realize now that we made a mistake in waiting so long to bring Kassy home. We thought we could spare her some of the pain. Now I realize that what Michael and I went through those first few weeks, pretending it wasn't true, is what Kassy had to go through alone in August. Maybe it would have been better for all of us to have done it together at once, but how do you know at the time?''

Kassy: ''Everyone has to choose their own way of handling things. I would never tell anyone to do it my way. It was just what I needed to do. For me, my dad's dying was like a play and I picked my part and played it as well as I could. I played the tough one, pretending it would all be over soon, he'd come home, and life would get back to normal.

''He knew what I was up to. He'd tease me when I'd go to the hospital and say, 'Kassy you can get mad in front of me. You can cry. I used to be mad about this too.' And I'd say to him, 'There's nothing to be mad about daddy. This will all be over soon.' I meant that the bad dream would be over, not that he'd die.''

Dr. Kubler-Ross says that many of the people she talked to refused to believe that they were dying, and that for some people, this is a necessary and helpful stage. Denying the truth is one method people use to protect themselves from shock, until a traumatic concept has a chance to mellow. Usually within a few days, or a few weeks, the truth does sink in.

For a few people, however, it is better never to face the truth. Some people die never having given up their belief that they are going to be cured. According to Dr. Kubler-Ross, however, this doesn't happen all that often. Most people first deny that they are going to die, and then get angry when they realize it is true. She calls this next stage ''anger.'' Most of the time, the people who are close to someone who is dying also go through a period of feeling angry.

It can break your heart when you think of what usually happens when someone who is dying gets mad. On one hand, it makes perfect sense. When people realize they are going to die, they also realize that they are going to lose all the people they love.

But whom do they take the anger out on? Usually, it's on the people they care about most, or on the nurses who are trying to make them comfortable. When family members don't understand what is happening — or when they do understand but can't take it any more — some try to find excuses for staying away. When they stay away, the person who is dying gets even more angry. ''I am dying and they don't even care.''

Florence: ''Michael was like that most of July. He was impossible. It's horrible to say, but he drove me up a wall. I wanted to be with him so much, to spend those last few months talking about the good times we'd had. But some days I'd go to the hospital and he'd tell me to leave. He'd shout at me to get out. I didn't understand that it meant he finally knew he was going to die. In one way I'm glad Kassy never saw any of this. She was his special one, and she idolized him.''

Kassy: ''By September, even I knew it was true. That was when I began to ask myself what kind of lousy God would take a man like my dad. Fifty-nine-years-old, just starting to think about retiring and having some time to spend with my mom. At night I'd beat up my Teddy bear, smash him against the wall. During the day I thought the doctors must be jerks; what did they mean there was *nothing* they could do? Then I'd hate myself for wanting to just hold him in my arms and cry forever...."

Dr. Kubler-Ross went on to describe what often happens next. She calls it "bargaining." The patient who is dying may say something like, "Okay, I get the picture, but please" — often the please is directed at God — "don't let me die until my son's wedding; until my daughter's baby is born; until the crocuses bloom in the spring."

It is a time of hope, of false dreams, and of families not knowing how to react. Should they go along with the bargains, or try to explain that they really don't make too much sense? Or are they making some bargains themselves, knowing all along that they are doing exactly that?

And anyway, is honesty always best? Would it be any better if no bargains were made? No one knows the answers to these questions, not even Dr. Elizabeth Kubler-Ross.

Kassy: "I promised myself that I'd never get angry again, that I'd be strong for him. If I could be strong, then he'd be okay. If I was weak, he'd die. But he'd say, 'Kassy you can cry. I know you want to cry'. And I'd tell him, 'Oh, no I don't.'

"By then, in September, I think he was way beyond any point I ever got to until almost a year later. By then, dying made some sort of weird sense to him. He tried to explain it to me once, but I couldn't understand."

Most professionals agree that families who try to talk about these questions — even when they have no answers—are able to cope with death a little better than families where what's happening is not talked about at all. Still, while it's true that today, more families are able to discuss death and dying than 30 years ago, not many are very good at it. Most people are still brought up to keep grief to themselves.

"Depression" is the name Dr. Kubler-Ross gives to the fourth stage of dying. It is the time for grief, for tears, and for despair. Psychiatrists and psychologists agree that while a dying person, or a relative, is depressed, it is not the time to try and cheer them up. It is the time to be silent, to hold someone's hand, or share someone's tears.

Kassy: "When school started, everything seemed to change for me. I got so moody. I couldn't concentrate. I'd be sitting in class and the teacher would call my name and it would take me a minute before I even knew what class I was in. Some of my teachers understood and stayed off my back, but a few of them made me feel like a fool in front of the whole class. They'd catch me staring out the window, or reading the wrong page.''

Florence: ''She was so quiet about it then, so sad those last few months before Michael died. I think it was easier for Barbara, Kassy's older sister. She could let herself fall apart; she spent most of those last months crying. Kassy would try to comfort her.

''For a while there, Kassy and I changed roles. She became the mother and I became the little girl, if that makes any sense. I guess I was more like Barbara than Kassy. I'd ask what to wear? What to cook? For a long time after Michael died, it was difficult for Kassy to go back to being the youngest child. I think Barbara and I went through a lot of our grief while Michael was dying .... Kassy, didn't start grieving until he had been dead for several months.''

You hear about people who are dying reaching the stage Dr. Kubler-Ross calls ''acceptance.'' They feel at peace with themselves and with the world. Sometimes, members of their family are able to accept it too, other times not. I don't think, however, that people accept death quite as often as professionals would like to believe. One thing that has always bothered me about the idea of acceptance is the unspoken implication that the dying person who *doesn't* find peace has failed, and that the family has somehow failed too. This happens frequently when someone is dying of cancer.

Kassy: ''I know that they all felt better about it than I did at the end. I just kept feeling worse and worse, and feeling guilty about that. Those last few weeks, I couldn't stand seeing him. I went to the hospital less and less. I couln't bear to see him slowly turning into someone I didn't know. I couldn't stand the way he would sometimes smile at me through the pain and the drugs they kept shooting into him. One day I'd be so mad. The next day I would be back to not believing it was true. The day after that I'd just lock myself in my room and cry.''

Cancer patients, and their families, often know for a number of months, sometimes for years, that death is inevitable.

When the process of dying goes on for so long, people sometimes go through Dr. Kubler-Ross's stages forward, or backward, and often more than once. Which stage, if any, a person happens to be in at the time of death, depends on many, many things.

The same stages sometimes start all over again for the family members after the person has died.

Kassy: "For six months I couldn't believe he was dead. It was as if he were just on another one of his business trips, coming home in two weeks. I'd hear a car pull into the driveway and I'd say to Barbara, 'Daddy's home.' When reality finally settled in, it was her turn to comfort me.

"I think part of me tried to keep busy so I'd have no time to think about the truth: he was dead. It's hard to explain because you'd think I would have wanted some time to myself to be able to see things clearly. But I preferred life to be a jumble.

"I'd offer to cook dinner. I'd bake chocolate chip cookies for Barbara. I remember one time she asked me why I never made chocolate cake. I went crazy; I told her to take the cookies and do you know what with them. I thought 'Dammit, get off my back. I'm only 15, just leave me the hell alone.' And yet, I had been the one to offer. I was the one who always wanted to keep busy, because when they did leave me alone, it was worse. When I had time on my hands, I could think clearly and I had to face the truth. It wasn't a play; he wasn't coming home. Then I'd go back to being busy all the time and my little fantasy would continue."

Florence: "I didn't know what to do with her. My heart would break. Why couldn't she accept it, at least realize that it was true? It made Barbara and me feel guilty. We had loved Michael too, but we knew it was time to get on with our own lives."

Kassy: "It's taken me almost year to get myself together. I'm getting back to my schoolwork a little more now. I think about him a little less — twice a day, instead of twice an hour. A month ago, I took his picture out of the drawer where I had put it the day he died. It took that long before I could get used to the idea of looking at him every day. I've never told anyone this before, but the day he died, I felt like throwing that photograph against the wall. It must be hard to understand why anyone would want to do that to someone they love so much, but I did. When he first died, I hated him for leaving me, as if it were his fault.''

Florence: ''Having someone you love die that way changes you forever. Part of you feels that you'll never be whole again, never know an hour of peace. Another part loses some of the ability to feel pain. Little things that used to be such a big deal to me don't seem so important anymore. I don't know if that contradiction makes any sense.''

Kassy: ''I carry a sadness in my heart. I wear it like someone else would wear a bracelet or a ring. Things strike me from a weird angle. To most people, butter pecan ice cream on a fall afternoon is just a treat. To me, it's what daddy was trying to eat one day the last week, biting off the bottom of the cone like a kid, sucking the butter pecan ice cream through as if it were a straw.

''Sometimes I read over the poems I've written and I wonder about loving and hating and how they can seem the same. But I know other kids who've had a mom or dad die of cancer and some of them say they know what I mean. It helps, you know, to find out that you're not the only weirdo who can't stand how she feels.''

In Canada, three out of every four people who die of cancer die in regular hospitals. Almost everyone else dies at home with very little, if any, support from professionals who have training in palliative care. No free-standing hospices are in operation, although several are being planned. Almost all palliative care units are affiliated with hospitals which also provide curative care. While almost 90,000 Canadians die of cancer each year, there are fewer than 275 beds in this entire country in hospital units dedicated solely to palliative care. Only 10 percent of Canadians who die of cancer receive any palliative care at all.

Some people, like Dr. Ley, argue further that palliative care does not work properly in a hospital setting, that a home-like atmosphere cannot be duplicated in a hospital, even a separate wing of a hospital, whose main focus is curative care. Dr. Ley, and the people who support her efforts, want to see more home care support programs in this country. They believe that many cancer patients could go home to die if their families could rely on the kind of community support that is becoming more commonplace in England and the U.S.

Perhaps the lack of facilities wouldn't be quite as hard to take if Canadians didn't know about the concept of palliative care. Perhaps if people like Dr. Elizabeth Kubler-Ross and Dame Cicely Saunders and programs in other countries hadn't shown us what is possible and filled us with hope, the lack of palliative care services in this country wouldn't grate quite so much.

But most Canadians who are trying to cope with a close relative or friend who is dying, have at least heard about this concept. Knowing what is being done in other countries makes it doubly hard for people who cannot do it themselves.

Florence: ''We didn't know what to do. Michael wanted so badly to come home for the end, to die in his own house. But we didn't have the money for nursing care 24 hours-a-day and that's what he needed.''

I have talked to many people who wish, with all their hearts, that they had time to think about emotions and the stages of dying. But there is so little time when there are so many practical decisions to be made.

Should someone who is dying be brought home? Hospital settings aren't exactly personal, but if a person who is dying does come home, how does a family cope? It seems horrible to be thinking about details like who will cook and who will clean when someone is dying. But these details have to be considered. Someone has to think about them.

Kassy: ''For me it was like therapy. I cooked and cleaned to keep from facing the truth. Someone I know, a friend whose mother was dying of breast cancer, resented having to do all the chores. All she ever talked about was 'getting the hell away'.''

Some families do try and bring the person who is dying back home. When they can get a bit of help from a day nurse, or a housekeeper, it often works pretty well. But more families I have talked to have had to send the dying person back to the hospital near the end. Caring for someone 24 hours-a-day is often too much for a family to bear.

Florence: "We couldn't have done it at the end. It's as simple as that. I can remember a few friends saying, 'You're going to let him come home, aren't you?' What a fantasy!"

People who are dying of cancer have special needs as the cancer cells begin to use up the nutrition that normal cells need. Cancer patients require special diets. Often they don't feel like eating, or can't keep many types of food down. Sometimes, they need pain-killers which can only be given by injection. Other times, they need help going to the bathroom — doing all the things we normally don't think about twice.

The saddest part, I think, is the guilt people sometimes feel about not being able to cope. Guilt is a word that came up often when I was speaking to people who loved someone who was dying of cancer.

Florence: "At first I did feel guilty. I knew coming home was what Michael really wanted. But people who aren't in the middle of all this don't understand. It's easy for them to say everyone should be able to die at home."

I spoke to people who were dying of cancer and felt guilty for being so helpless. I spoke to people who were trying to help them who felt guilty about not helping enough.

My impression was that teenagers feel the most guilt of all. Those are the years when it is time to explore the world, to feel proud of newly found independence, to break loose. At the same time, it is time to begin to share part of the burden. One day you want to, the next day you don't.

The pages you have just been reading took a year to write.

Should I even include a section on death and dying in this book, I kept asking myself? Once I decided that I was right to have done it, I started to wonder if I should have mentioned concepts like palliative care or people like Dr. Elizabeth Kubler-Ross.

"What if...?" I kept asking this same question of every doctor and social worker I talked to about this part of the book, "What if kids trying to cope with someone who has cancer read about all the problems other kids are having — with grief, guilt, and anger — and they're not having any problems at all? What if they read what I write and end up thinking there's something wrong with them for feeling okay? What if they end up, *because of what I write,* experiencing guilt?''

I worried about this for weeks. And then the weeks became months and I started dreaming about it. It got to the point where I was so worried that I wrote nothing, not a word. I couldn't finish this book.

This went on until one day I met Dr. Stephen Fleming, a psychology professor at Toronto's York University.

''I'm not getting anywhere,'' I told him. ''I'm doing nothing but worrying about causing kids a lot of grief.''

Dr. Fleming smiled as he told me very simply, ''Of all the things you have to worry about, you don't have to worry about that!

''A few kids,'' he continued, *''a very few* kids will go through the experience of someone they care about dying of cancer and get through it without too much grief.

''They'll read what other kids have to say and feel lucky. The rest, you know, all go through the same things we adults go through, only often, it's worse. It can only help kids to find out that other people are feeling the same way.''

I thought about it and began to realize that what Dr. Fleming was saying made sense. The 50 kids I had talked to over an 18-month period had indeed had very similar things to say about what it's like to love someone who is dying or someone who has died already.

I began to realize that there had been times during those months that I could have finished any sentence that someone had begun.

''You won't believe it,'' someone would start out, and because I had heard it before, I knew by the tone in the forlorn voice that I was about to hear again how guilty someone felt for being angry. ''I got so mad at him for getting sick. How can you be mad at someone with cancer who is going to die?''

But I heard it more times than I can count. The teenagers I talked to shared so many feelings. I wished at times that they all could have met to trade stories. That way, they would have known for sure that almost everyone feels neglected and overprotected at the same time.

I thought about one high school student in particular who felt neglected one week and utterly nagged the next. "How can it be that one minute my parents act as if they couldn't care less about what I do and the next minute they're breathing down my neck?"

It was a good question — how can it be?

I asked a few of their parents. "Your kids say you're driving them nuts. They talk about the hard times they are having. Can you see it? Are you acting a bit weird?"

Mostly I got gestures rather than answers. Hands thrown up in the air, sighs, and tear-filled eyes that looked as if they wanted to drift off into space rather than face the answers to those questions.

"How can I tell my daughter that I'm coming apart at the seams?" a man whose wife was dying of stomach cancer asked me. "She needs me to be strong, and I feel as if I'm six-years-old. Are you crazy? Of course I'm acting weird."

In the 1960s, doctors like Elizabeth Kubler-Ross made up labels like bargaining and denial, but ordinary people have been *living* these labels for many, many years. Mothers have been acting like their young daughters, fathers like young sons. But what may be worse for parents is that they probably feel doubly guilty when they cannot be strong. Parents wish they knew what to do, what to say, and how to protect you from the worst. With the best of intentions, they sometimes don't give you what you need.

What's the point of saying all this? The point was made by another doctor I spoke to, Dr. Saul Levine, chief of psychiatry at Toronto's Sunnybrook Hospital.

"Saul," I said to him just before leaving his office, "tell me, is hearing all this stuff really going to help these kids?"

He thought for a few seconds before he answered: "Every time I have been faced with looking at who is the most helpful person in a crisis, any kind of crisis, I have usually found that it's other people who are going through the same thing, or have gone through it before.

"Everyone seems to have the same feeling: 'God, if I tell people how I feel, they'll think I'm off my rocker.' I hear this all the time. But, if people hear what they themselves are thinking from someone else in the same boat, they believe that they're not alone. It's different, often much better, than hearing it from a doctor. You find out that it's normal to feel whatever you do feel. It's a wonderful thing to discover that you're not nuts, or alone!''

Perhaps your own situation is completely different from Kassy's, but you *feel* the same way. Or, maybe the scene is the same, but the players are different. Never mind. The point is, I think, the very one Dr. Levine repeated as I left. ''When someone you love is dying of cancer, it's normal to feel whatever you do feel.''

Somewhere, I guarantee it, someone else knows exactly what you're going through.

PART II
The Common Cancers

The Carcinomas

Carcinomas are cancers which begin in epithelial cells. These are the cells which line the inside and outside surfaces of the different organs of the body.

Skin Cancer

What is the skin?

The skin is a huge organ which protects the body from injury, excretes waste products, and regulates body temperature.

What is skin cancer?

Like other carcinomas, skin cancer develops in epithelial cells that form the lining of the skin. There are three main types of epithelial skin cells: basal cells, squamous cells, and melanoma cells. Skin cancer can start to grow in any of these three types of skin cells.

Who gets skin cancer and what is the outlook?

Skin cancer is the most common type of cancer; each year in Canada, about 17,000 new cases are diagnosed. About 95% of them begin in either squamous, or basal cells, and because they

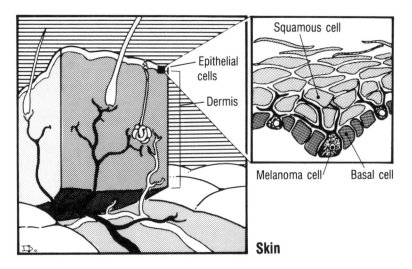

Skin

are slow-growing and tend not to spread, are completely curable almost 100% of the time.

Malignant melanoma, the one type of skin cancer that is difficult to treat, grows and spreads quickly. Fortunately, it is rare and can be cured when it is detected at an early stage. Malignant melanoma is diagnosed in approximately 1,200 Canadians each year, almost two-thirds of whom can be cured.

What causes skin cancer and who is at high risk?

Skin cancer is most often caused by long-term over-exposure to the ultraviolet rays of the sun, although some chemical pollutants can cause it as well. For this reason, cancer of the skin tends to show up on areas of the body — the face, the backs of the hands — that are exposed to the environment. Because these areas are also visible, skin cancer rarely remains undetected for long.

Dark-skinned people whose skin cells contain large amounts of melanin, which filters out ultraviolet rays, are less susceptible to skin cancer than light-skinned people.

Farmers, fishermen, and sailors, who work in the sun, as well as avid sunbathers, also tend to get skin cancer more frequently than other people.

The signs and symptoms of skin cancer

The easier-to-cure types of skin cancer usually show up as pale, waxlike, pearly nodules or red, scaly patches.

Malignant melanoma usually starts out as a small, mole-like growth which then begins to get bigger, and changes colour, or shape. Sometimes, a malignant melanoma will itch.

The diagnosis of skin cancer

Suspicious-looking skin conditions are biopsied incisionally if they are large, and excisionally if they are small. This minor surgical procedure can usually be performed in a doctor's office with only a local anaesthetic. The biopsy is then sent to a lab to be examined for cancerous cells.

The treatment of skin cancer

Surgery, radiation, electrodesiccation, and cryosurgery are used to treat the two common types of skin cancer. Electrodesiccation destroys tissue by using heat. Cryosurgery destroys tissue by freezing it.

Surgery is the most common treatment for malignant melanoma, although radiation therapy or chemotherapy are sometimes used when it has spread.

Lung Cancer

What are the lungs?

The lungs are a pair of elastic organs that are used for breathing.

What is lung cancer?

Lung cancer is a carcinoma that generally develops in the epithelial cells that form the interior lining of the airways to the lungs. This is because the airways get the most exposure to inhaled pollutants; almost everyone who develops this type of lung cancer smokes. A rarer type of lung cancer can begin in the epithelial cells of the "outlying" regions of a lung; non-smokers sometimes get this type of lung cancer.

Who gets lung cancer and what is the outlook?

Lung cancer kills more Canadians than any other kind of cancer. During 1984, approximately 10,000 Canadians will

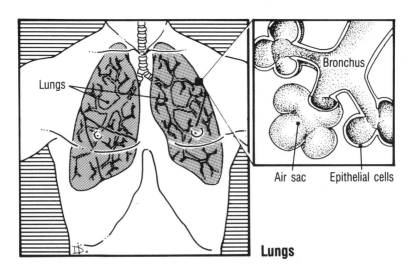

Lungs

learn that they have lung cancer and about 9,600 will die of this disease. These numbers have been increasing, especially among females. Lung cancer is the leading cause of death from cancer in males, and researchers are predicting that it will also be the leading cause of death from cancer in females within a couple of years.

The overall prognosis for lung cancer — a medical term that describes what will probably happen to one person, given what has already happened to others in the same situation — is bleak. More than 90% of lung cancer patients die within five years.

If a former lung cancer patient is alive and symptom-free five years after treatment, it is unlikely that cancerous lung cells will reappear, and these rare individuals are considered to be cured.

What causes lung cancer and who is at high risk?

Smoking is the main cause of lung cancer. The more and longer a person smokes, the greater the risk of developing lung cancer. More than 90% of lung cancer patients are smokers.

People who have smoked a pack or more of cigarettes a day for many years — perhaps as many as 20 — have the greatest risk of developing lung cancer. According to some studies, a person who starts smoking at age 15, is 30 times more likely to develop lung cancer by age 35 than someone who has never smoked.

People who are exposed to asbestos, chromium, nickel, coal tars or radioactive uranium — usually because of their jobs — also have a higher-than-average risk of developing lung cancer. Non-smokers are less affected by these substances than smokers.

Lung cancer can be prevented. The best protection is to never start smoking. The next best protection is to quit if you already smoke. When a person stops smoking, his or her risk of developing lung cancer stops increasing. Ten to 15 years after quitting, a former smoker, even a former long-term, heavy smoker, has almost the same risk of developing lung cancer as a person who has never smoked.

Inhaling smoke and other pollutants year after year damages

the cleaning mechanism of the lungs. When the lungs can no longer clean themselves properly, inhaled carcinogenic substances build up and may eventually cause a gene to mutate. Some people smoke for years, however, and never get lung cancer. It may be that their lungs are better than other people's at resisting the effects of these carcinogenic substances.

The signs and symptoms of lung cancer

Lung cancer is usually suspected when someone coughs up blood or complains of a hacking cough that continues to get worse; the lungs are trying to get rid of the foreign object — the tumour — that is lodged in an airway. If the tumour is large enough, it can obstruct the passageway almost completely and the patient will also experience chest pain and difficulty breathing.

The diagnosis of lung cancer

When symptoms such as these persist, an X-ray of the lungs is taken to determine if there is a tumour and where it is located. Usually some sputum — the technical term for spit — is examined for any cancer cells that the tumour may have shed. Often, the doctor will examine the airway with a bronchoscope, a type of endoscope that can be inserted into the airway via the mouth. Using a bronchoscope, the doctor can examine the airway for a tumour and, if there is one, take a biopsy of it. This biopsy will be sent to the lab for microscopic examination.

If the tumour is too far along a bronchial tube to be reached with a bronchoscope, it is more difficult to take a biopsy. A fine needle is inserted through the chest wall, using a special type of X-ray for guidance.

If the doctor suspects that nearby lymph nodes have trapped some cells shed by the tumour, a minor surgical procedure will be performed. A tube will be passed through a tiny slit above the breast bone, and a biopsy of a lymph node will be taken and examined in the lab.

If these lymph nodes contain cancer cells, other tests will likely be performed to determine the extent to which the cancer has spread to more distant organs.

The treatment of lung cancer

There are many decisions to be made once a diagnosis of lung cancer is confirmed. Some lung cancers grow and spread very quickly; others grow relatively slowly and tend not to spread for a long time.

Surgery, radiation therapy, or chemotherapy, and sometimes a combination of the three, can be used to treat lung cancer.

If the tumour is localized to one particular spot, it can often be removed surgically. Unfortunately, only about one in five lung cancer patients are diagnosed when their tumours are still localized; of these, fewer than one in four are still alive five years after their initial diagnosis is made.

If the patient has other problems which preclude surgery, or if the tumour is not in an easy-to-reach place, radiation therapy is sometimes used.

If there is evidence that the tumour has spread to distant parts of the body, chemotherapy is sometimes used. Over the past few years, there have been some good results using chemotherapy on patients with certain types of lung cancer.

In many cases, lung cancer is detected at such an advanced stage that only palliative care is feasible.

Breast Cancer

What is the breast?

The breast is a gland designed to secrete milk. It remains small in males, enlarges in females during adolescence, and enlarges even further during pregnancy and when milk is produced. People tend to think of a breast as a single gland but, in fact, each breast consists of between 15 to 20 lobes, or segments. Each section has a duct, and each duct opens onto the nipple.

What is breast cancer?

Most breast cancers begin in the epithelial cells that line the milk ducts and milk sacs. Some breast cancers grow into the duct canal; others grow into the breast tissue itself.

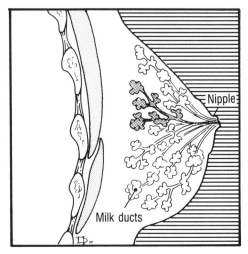

Breast

Who gets breast cancer and what is the outlook?

Every year, approximately 9,400 Canadian women develop breast cancer, and approximately 3,700 women die of this disease. One in every 12 Canadian women will develop breast cancer at some point during her life. The disease is rare in women under the age of 30 and becomes more common after the age of 40. Occasionally, breast cancer develops in males, although it is usually detected early on and successfully treated.

Breast cancer in females can also be successfully treated in many cases. If it is detected when it is still localized, it can be cured 85% of the time.

Once breast cancer has spread to the lymph nodes nearby, at which point it is referred to as invasive breast cancer with regional involvement, the chances of a cure fall to slightly higher than 50%.

For breast cancer that is advanced when diagnosed, the outlook is usually grim.

While more Canadian women are developing breast cancer than in the past, about the same number of women are dying from this disease each year. This means that treatment is successful in more cases.

When approximately 16 years have passed, a former breast cancer patient is considered cured.

What causes breast cancer and who is at high risk?

Although scientists do not know the exact cause of breast cancer, diets that are high in fat are thought to increase a person's risk of developing this type of carcinoma. In countries like Japan where people have a low-fat diet, the incidence of breast cancer is also low. In North America, the diet is generally high in fat and the incidence of breast cancer is also high.

The female sex hormone estrogen — which is contained in birth control pills — has been linked to breast cancer in animals. There is, however, no general link between the pill and breast cancer in humans. Women who are interested in taking birth control pills are advised to discuss the advantages and disadvantages of this method of birth control with a doctor, and to take as low a dose as possible.

Certain women seem to be more prone to breast cancer than other women.

A woman who has had breast cancer once has a greater chance of developing it again than a woman who has never had the disease. The higher risk may be caused by environmental factors such as diet which do not change.

A woman who has more than one close relative with breast cancer — a mother and a sister, for example, — has a higher-than-average risk of developing this disease than a woman whose family has no history of breast cancer. Researchers are not certain whether this is due to hereditary or environmental factors, but many researchers blame environmental factors.

Women who have had a first child before the age of 25 seem to develop breast cancer less often than women who bear their first child after the age of 30, or women who have no children at all. Researchers do not understand why this is so.

Women who begin menstruating before the age of 11, or continue to menstruate after the age of 50, also tend to have a higher-than-average risk of developing this disease.

Some studies show that overweight, post-menopausal women develop breast cancer more frequently than women whose weight is normal.

Other studies show that women who have a history of non-malignant, or benign, breast tumours, also have a higher-than-average risk of developing cancerous breast tumours.

The signs and symptoms of breast cancer

When a woman has breast cancer, there are usually no obvious symptoms, such as pain. When the tumour grows into a duct, however, there may be discharge or bleeding from a nipple.

Breast cancer surveillance

There are several ways of detecting breast cancer at an early stage. The easiest is through breast self-examination, usually called BSE. All women should practise BSE, but women over the age of 35 in a high risk group should also discuss the other available surveillance tests for breast cancer with a doctor. These tests include mammography and ultrasonography. Researchers are also working on a diagnostic blood test for breast cancer and it is hoped that this simple type of test will be available to the public within a few years.

Studies have shown that women who do BSE properly can detect early breast tumours that are no larger than the size of a pea. Women who discover breast tumours "by accident" often find tumours the size of a golf ball. The Canadian Cancer Society distributes free pamphlets that show women how to do BSE. It is completely painless and takes no more than a couple of minutes each month. Many women also ask a doctor to do BSE for them, and to make sure that they themselves are doing it properly.

A low-radiation level X-ray called a mammogram is also used to detect early breast cancers in women who have stopped menstruating. For a number of years, this type of X-ray was used on premenopausal women as well. The studies that were done to evaluate mammography on premenopausal women, however, showed that it wasn't particularly helpful, and better methods of mammography are now being investigated by the Canadian National Breast-Screening Study.

In some research centres, ultrasound waves which can detect breast tumours because they have a different density than normal breast tissue, are being used to detect breast cancer at an early stage.

The diagnosis of breast cancer

Any lump in a breast should be examined by a doctor immediately. If the lump appears to be a cyst — a sac filled with liquid — the area around the cyst can be frozen with a local anaesthetic, and the fluid removed with a thin needle.

This fluid is sent to a lab and if its cells are benign, which they are more than nine times out of 10, no further treatment is necessary.

Solid masses, however, must be biopsied.

Sometimes a biopsy can be taken in the doctor's office. The area is frozen with a local anaesthetic, a tiny incision is made, and a piece of tissue is removed. Other times, a needle aspiration can be performed; a bit of tissue is removed by using a thin needle which sucks up a bit of the tumour.

In most cases, however, a general anaesthetic followed by a surgical procedure are necessary. Often, the biopsy is sent to the lab while the patient remains under general anaesthetic. This is done so that if further surgery is required, the patient will not have to undergo a general anaesthetic twice. More than eight out of 10 solid tumours turn out to be benign.

The treatment of breast cancer

Surgery, radiation therapy, chemotherapy — and frequently a combination of all three — are used to treat cancerous breast tumours.

While surgery is still the most common treatment, the disfiguring radical mastectomy is no longer frequently performed. Instead of ressecting the cancerous tumour along with the entire breast, all the lymph nodes in the area of the breast, and the muscle underneath the breast — for that is what radical breast surgery involves — much less is surgically removed.

The least radical type of breast surgery is lumpectomy. The tumour, a margin of normal breast tissue as a preventive measure, and usually a number of nearby lymph nodes are ressected. The lymph nodes are examined in the lab for cancerous cells.

Sometimes, the entire breast is removed — a simple mastectomy — and perhaps some lymph nodes, but nothing else.

Other times, the breast, some tissue of the armpit, and perhaps some lymph nodes, but not the muscle, are removed. This procedure is called a modified radical mastectomy.

When radiation therapy is used, the tumour is exposed to destructive cobalt rays.

If cancer cells from a breast tumour have already metastasized from the primary tumour, chemotherapy is frequently used.

Adjuvant chemotherapy is now also frequently used immediately after surgery or radiation therapy, *before* there is any sign of a secondary tumour. The aim of adjuvant chemotherapy is to kill any shed cells before they have a chance to grow into a secondary tumour. The results of the initial studies on adjuvant chemotherapy are not yet complete, but some doctors feel that better cure rates are going to show up with this adjuvant use of chemotherapy for breast cancer.

Hormone therapy is also sometimes used for certain types of breast cancer that depend on a particular hormonal environment to grow.

Sometimes, if the hormonal balance can be changed, by either adding or subtracting hormones, a cancerous breast tumour will shrink, instead of growing.

To reduce the amount of a particular hormone, the organ that produces the hormone is removed surgically or destroyed by radiation. The ovaries, for example, produce estrogen and are sometimes ressected or destroyed by radiation. Drugs can also be given to inhibit the production of hormones.

If more of a certain hormone is required, it can be given by pills or injections.

After the treatment

Many former breast cancer patients have emotional problems to face.

Although most women who have had a breast removed can return to normal activities within a few weeks, some find that the fear of what life will be like with only one breast is overwhelming. A common worry is that the man in her life will no longer find her attractive. Or, if single, a woman may worry about being able to begin a relationship with a new man.

Some relationships do break up because of breast cancer, although most do not. And women who have had mastectomies do find they can begin new relationships.

The Canadian Cancer Society has created a nationwide support service called the Mastectomy Visiting Program for women who have recently undergone treatment for breast cancer. Many women find it helpful to talk to someone who has shared the same experience. Other women want information about artificial breast forms, or exercises that can help them cope with the recovery process.

Reconstructive surgery to replace a missing breast, called mammoplasty, is becoming more and more common. People who used to scoff at women who were so concerned about replacing a lost breast are finally beginning to believe that, for some women, mammoplasty is beneficial, and even necessary.

Prostate Cancer

What is the prostate?

The prostate is a gland that is part of the male reproductive system. It produces secretions that are important in the make-up of the semen.

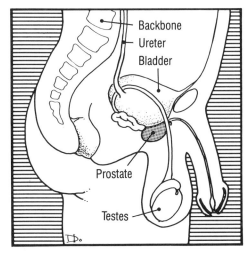

Prostate

What is prostate cancer?

Prostate cancer is a slow-growing cancer which generally begins to develop in the epithelial cells of the lining of the back of the prostate gland.

Who gets prostate cancer and what is the outlook?

The number of Canadian men who get cancer of the prostate gland is second only to the number who get lung cancer. Unlike lung cancer, the chances of treating prostate cancer successfully are high. Of the 6,200 Canadian men who get prostate cancer each year, about 70% can be successfully treated.

One of the reasons why so many prostate cancer patients survive is that it is one of the slowest growing of all cancers and most prostate cancer patients are over the age of 65 when a tumour is first detected. In fact, the disease is sometimes only discovered when a person dies of something totally unrelated and an autopsy is performed, revealing the presence of a cancerous prostate tumour.

Often, however, prostate cancer can be life threatening. After a number of years, cells from prostate cancer tumours usually spread into the lymph nodes nearby, or to other parts of the body via the bloodstream.

What causes prostate cancer and who is at high risk?

The causes and risk factors for prostate cancer are unknown.

The signs and symptoms of prostate cancer

Cancerous prostate tumours often cause no signs or symptoms at all. When there are symptoms, they are usually much the same as those associated with a more common, but benign, prostate problem in which the organ becomes swollen. They include: difficulty in urinating, frequent urination, blood in the urine, continuing low back pain, or pain in the pelvis or upper thighs.

The diagnosis of prostate cancer

When prostate cancer is suspected, the doctor will examine the area digitally — using a finger — through the rectum. If a tumour is felt, minor surgery will be performed to take a biopsy and usually a brief hospital stay will be necessary. If the biopsy reveals cancerous cells, more tests will likely be done to determine if the prostate cancer has spread and if so, to what extent.

The treatment of prostate cancer

Surgery, radiation therapy, and hormone therapy, and sometimes a combination of all three are used to treat prostate cancer. Chemicals, other than hormones, are rarely used.

If the tumour has not yet spread beyond the gland itself — and especially if the patient is elderly — treatment can sometimes be postponed because prostate cancer grows so slowly. If the patient is experiencing uncomfortable symptoms, however, the prostate, or at least the part of it that contains the tumour, can be removed.

If the tumour is localized, it can sometimes be reduced by radiation therapy.

Hormone treatment is often used when the cancer has metastasized to other parts of the body. Sometimes the testes, which produce male hormones and promote prostate tumour growth, are removed. Other times, female hormones are injected to counterbalance the male hormones.

Hormone treatment for prostate cancer can produce unpleasant side effects. Some of these drugs cause impotence — the loss of the ability to have sexual intercourse.

Hormone therapy can also cause the patient's breasts to become enlarged, although radiating the breasts prior to hormone therapy can prevent this uncomfortable side effect.

Stomach Cancer

What is the stomach?

The stomach is a muscular, pear-shaped bag that conveys food from the esophagus to the intestines. The stomach operates like a washing machine. The food is the laundry and when it enters the stomach, gastric juices pour in like water. When the stomach churns the food, the gastric juices mix with it to form chyme.

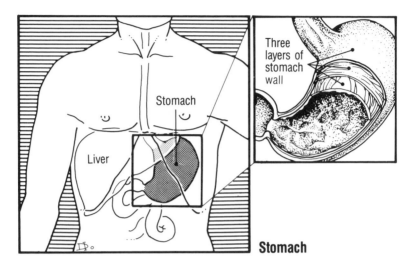

Stomach

What is stomach cancer?

Cancer of the stomach is a carcinoma that develops in the epithelial cells of the innermost layer of the stomach wall's three layers. The tumour spreads from this inner layer towards the outer layers. When it metastasizes, stomach cancer tends to spread through the bloodstream to the liver or lungs, and through the lymphatic system to the lymph nodes nearby. Sometimes stomach cancer also spreads to nearby organs such as the pancreas or the spleen.

At one time, stomach cancer was a major cause of death in Canada. Over the past couple of decades, however, the incidence of stomach cancer has declined and is continuing to decline.

Who gets stomach cancer and what is the outlook?

Approximately 2,600 Canadians develop cancer of the stomach each year. Almost two-thirds of these people are men, mostly over the age of 55.

Cancer of the stomach is more common among people in low-income groups. Researchers speculate that this may be due to the fact that people in low-income groups tend to eat fewer fresh fruits and vegetables and more preserved foods than people in higher income brackets.

When it is detected at an early stage — before it has invaded more than two of the three layers of the stomach wall — stomach cancer can be successfully treated. Unfortunately, early detection is rare and every year, approximately 2,300 Canadians die of this disease.

About five years after treatment is stopped, surviving stomach cancer patients are considered cured.

What causes stomach cancer and who is at high risk?

While the incidence of stomach cancer has been declining in North America, it has remained high in other countries. Scientists have not been able to discover the exact reason for this because many things about the causes of cancer are still a mystery. Most researchers, however, believe that a high use, over many years, of preservatives such as nitrates and nitrites, along with a low consumption of fresh foods, particularly fruit and vegetables containing vitamin C, increase a person's risk of developing stomach cancer.

Entire populations of countries where people's diets are high in preservatives and low in fresh fruit and vegetables have a higher-than-average risk of developing stomach cancer. Ten times as many Japanese as Canadians, for example, develop stomach cancer. The lack of refrigeration in Japan until recently, resulted in the high use of preservatives, and low use of fresh fruit and vegetables. This is the reason most scientists give for the high rate of stomach cancer in that country.

People who have had stomach surgery for ulcers or have suffered from a particular kind of anemia (called pernicious anemia), or achlorhydria (a lack of hydrochloric acid in the stomach), tend to have a higher-than-average risk of developing stomach cancer.

The signs and symptoms of stomach cancer

One of the problems in detecting stomach cancer at an early stage is that the symptoms are usually vague. Even by the time stomach cancer has reached an advanced stage, most people complain only of mild stomach pain, a slight feeling of nausea, or persistent heartburn. When there are more definite signs and symptoms, they are usually fatigue, vomiting, blood in the stools, or rapid weight loss.

Surveillance for stomach cancer

Because of its high rate of stomach cancer, Japan has developed better methods for early diagnosis of this disease. The Japanese now conduct mass screening programs for stomach cancer just as we, in North America, conduct mass screening programs for cancer of the cervix and the breast. The Japanese test tens of thousands of people every year by examining their stomachs with barium X-rays. Some Japanese studies have shown that stomach cancer can be cured 95% of the time when it is detected at an early stage.

Because the rate of stomach cancer in Canada is low, it is not practical to conduct mass screening programs. What we could do, but don't, is screen people who have a higher-than-average risk of developing this disease.

The diagnosis of stomach cancer

When stomach cancer is suspected, an X-ray of the stomach is taken to determine if there is a tumour and its location.

If it looks as if there is a tumour, the patient is sedated, and a gastroscope is inserted through the mouth into the stomach. The doctor examines the stomach for a tumour and, if there is one, a biopsy is taken.

Sometimes, a tiny piece of tissue is nipped off the tumour and biopsied; other times, cells are simply scraped off the surface of the tumour with a tiny brush. The biopsy is then sent to a lab for examination.

The treatment of stomach cancer

The treatment for stomach cancer is surgery. The tumour is removed and part, or all, of the stomach is generally removed as well. Sometimes the spleen is removed if it is suspected that the original tumour has spread to this nearby organ.

When it is obvious that the disease has metastasized, chemotherapy is sometimes added to the treatment in the hope of stopping, or at least slowing down, the spreading process.

Stomach cancer patients can live an almost normal life without a stomach. When the stomach is removed, eating a number of small meals per day is usually enough to control digestive problems. Many cancer patients who have lost their stomachs also find that a low carbohydrate, high protein diet is helpful. Most people also take injections of vitamin B12.

Cancer of the Testes (Testicles)

What are the testes?

The two testes, or testicles, are the male sex organs that produce sperm, the cells that fertilize the female egg. They are oval-shaped organs which are suspended in a pouch, called the scrotum.

What is cancer of the testes?

Cancer of the testes, which is sometimes called testicular cancer, is a carcinoma which develops in the epithelial cells that line the testicles.

The idea of having testicular cancer is very scary to many men who think that they will automatically lose the ability to father children, or to have sexual intercourse at all. This is not usually true. Almost all cancers of the testicle involve only one of the two organs and a man who has only one testicle can have sex, or father children, as easily as a man with two.

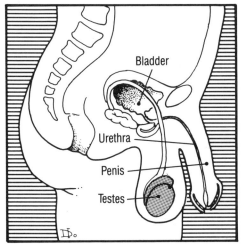

Testes

Who gets cancer of the testes and what is the outlook?

Fewer than 400 Canadian men get cancer of the testicles every year. Most of them are between the ages of 25 and 40 and almost 90% can be cured.

Five years after treatment, surviving testicular cancer patients are considered cured.

What causes testicular cancer and who is at high risk?

Although the exact causes of testicular cancer are unknown, researchers have been able to show that men whose brothers or fathers have had testicular cancer are more likely to develop the disease than men in whose families there has been no history of testicular cancer.

The testes are formed inside the body near the kidneys and normally, they descend into the scrotum shortly after birth. Men whose testicles never descend, or descend after the age of six, also have a higher-than-average risk of developing testicular cancer.

The signs and symptoms of testicular cancer

Testicular cancer is usually discovered when a swelling, or a hard lump, is noticed in a testicle. Sometimes, the patient is also aware of a dull ache in the abnominal area and, if the tumour is growing quickly, there may be sharp pain. Some patients' breasts become enlarged; others develop tender nipples. The symptoms are due to a change in hormone production caused by the tumour.

The diagnosis of testicular cancer

When a testicular tumour is suspected, the doctor will first examine the testicle. If a tumour can be felt, further tests are usually performed to determine if the disease has metastasized. A blood test for this purpose has recently been developed. A biopsy is rarely taken for this type of carcinoma.

The treatment of testicular cancer

Surgery, radiation therapy, and chemotherapy are all used in the treatment of testicular cancer.

Testicular tumours are first removed surgically and then cells are examined to determine if they are cancerous. Sometimes nearby lymph nodes are surgically removed as well.

Radiation therapy and chemotherapy are also sometimes used to treat localized testicular cancers as well as those that have spread.

Oral Cancer

What is oral cancer?

Oral cancers are a group of cancers that develop in the epithelial cells of the tissues that line the mouth: lips; gums; floor of the mouth; tongue; salivary glands; tonsils; and back of the throat, called the pharynx. Because of their location, oral cancers are usually detected at an early stage, patients themselves being the best detectives. When oral cancers spread, however, they tend to move into the lymph nodes of the neck and sometimes into the bones nearby.

Who gets oral cancer and what is the outlook?

Approximately 2,750 Canadians develop one of the different types of oral cancer each year. Oral cancers rarely develop in young people; the vast majority of oral cancer patients are over 60-years-old.

When they are detected early, most oral cancers can be treated

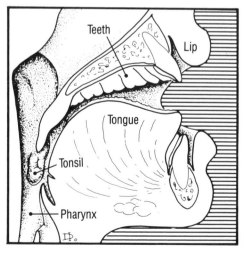

Mouth

successfully. The 700 Canadians who die from this disease each year are mostly those whose cancers were not detected at an early stage.

Five years after treatment is stopped, surviving oral cancer patients are considered cured.

What causes oral cancer and who is at high risk?

While the exact cause of oral cancer is unknown, scientists do know that the disease is not contagious in any way. No one has caught oral cancer from touching or kissing someone who does have it.

Studies are beginning to suggest that certain chemicals, nutrients, and hormones encourage oral cancers to develop. From studies such as these, scientists have been able to show that some people have a higher-than-average risk of developing this disease.

People who develop cancer of the mouth, for example, are four times more likely to be smokers than non-smokers. People who smoke pipes or cigars develop lip cancer more frequently than non-smokers.

The ultraviolet rays of the sun can also cause cancer to develop on the lips. People who work or play in the sun for long periods of time can protect themselves from lip cancer by using a sunscreen containing PABA, or a sunblock containing either zinc oxide or titanium dioxide.

Heavy drinkers of alcohol develop oral cancer more frequently than people who don't drink at all, or drink moderately. If a person smokes *and* drinks heavily, the chances of developing oral cancer are even higher.

Few people chew tobacco these days, but studies done in the southern U.S. where this habit is still popular have linked it to oral cancer.

Betel-nut chewing, a habit popular among Asians, has also been linked to oral cancer.

The signs and symptoms of oral cancer

Oral cancer is not generally painful at an early stage. It usually shows up as sores that either don't heal properly or bleed easily.

Sometimes, a precancerous condition called leukoplakia develops prior to an oral cancer. The signs of leukoplakia are white, or red and white, areas inside the mouth.

The diagnosis of oral cancer

Although most suspicious spots in or around the mouth turn out to be benign, any sore that persists for several weeks should be examined by a dentist or a doctor.

If a sore does look suspicious, a biopsy will be performed and cells from it will be sent to a lab for microscopic examination.

The treatment of oral cancer

Surgery, radiation therapy, and sometimes a combination of the two are used in the treatment of oral cancer.

When radiation therapy is chosen, the patient generally experiences uncomfortable side effects for a number of months. They sometimes lose their sense of taste and experience a condition called dry mouth, because radiation temporarily destroys the cells produced by the saliva glands. The teeth usually become loosened and for this reason, a dentist is generally part of the treatment team. Rest and good nutrition are particularly important for patients undergoing treatment for oral cancer.

Sometimes, if the doctor believes that an oral cancer has metastasized, the lymph nodes near the cancer site are radiated as well. There are also times when cosmetic surgery is necessary, but this is not usual. Most oral cancers are detected early enough so that there is very little scarring of the face as a result of treatment.

Cancer of the Colon and the Rectum (Colorectal Cancer)

What are the colon and the rectum?

The colon, which is also called the large intestine or large bowel, is a long, hollow organ whose job it is to remove the liquid from undigested food. By the time the waste that remains gets to the final portion of the colon, called the rectum, it is in the form that we recognize as a normal stool, or bowel movement. At the very end of the rectum is the anus, a muscular valve which can be controlled.

The wall, or lining, of the colon is made up of epithelial cells which actually absorb this liquid. The epithelial cells also produce mucus which lubricates the passageway. If the passageway is irritated for some reason, the epithelial cells will produce more mucus to reduce the irritation.

What is colorectal cancer?

Cancers of the colon and rectum are usually talked about as one type of cancer called colorectal cancer. They develop in the epithelial cells that line the interior of the large intestine and the rectum.

Who gets colorectal cancer and what is the outlook?

Colorectal cancer is diagnosed in about 10,300 Canadians each year, mostly over the age of 50. Unlike many cancers that are associated with sex organs or lifestyles that are more common to either men or women, colorectal cancers develop fairly evenly among males and females.

When it is detected at an early stage, the outlook for cancer of the colon is good; 70% of patients can be cured. Once cancer

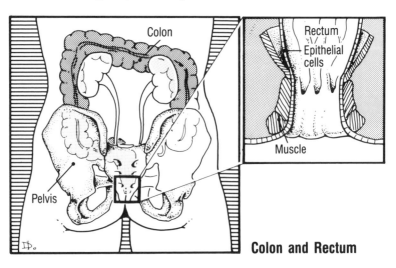

Colon and Rectum

of the colon has spread beyond the intestine into the nearby lymph nodes, however, the chances of survival fall to about one in three.

Cancer of the rectum is less optimistic. Only half of the people whose cancer of the rectum is still localized when it is diagnosed can be cured, and once it has metastasized, the outlook is grim.

Each year, approximately 5,500 Canadian men and women die of this disease.

Surviving colorectal cancer patients are considered cured five years after treatment is stopped.

What causes colorectal cancer and who is at high risk?

While the exact cause of colorectal cancer is unknown, scientists have been learning more about the risk factors for this type of carcinoma in recent years.

People whose diets are high in fat and low in citrus fruit and certain vegetables like cabbage and cauliflower, tend to have a higher-than-average risk of developing colorectal cancer. Recent studies have shown that a diet high in animal fat destroys the epithelial cells of the colon which must then be regenerated. If calcium is added to this high fat diet, however, epithelial cells are not destroyed. This may possibly mean that a diet high in animal fat has a different effect than a diet high in milk fat, although no studies have as yet been conducted on humans.

Scientists believe that small, non-cancerous growths called benign polyps that develop in the epithelial tissues of the intestines can eventually become cancerous if they are not removed.

People who have had colorectal cancer once have a higher-than-average risk of developing it a second time, and people whose close relatives have had this disease also seem to develop it more frequently than people with no family history of colorectal cancer. Epidemiologists are not certain whether this has to do with hereditary factors or environmental factors such as diet, but more and more research is pointing to dietary factors.

The signs and symptoms of colorectal cancer

Most of the symptoms for colorectal cancer are the same as the symptoms for other intestinal problems. A change in bowel habits is the most common symptom, but any bleeding, or obvious amounts of mucus in the stools, should be checked right away.

The diagnosis of colorectal cancer

When cancer of the colon or rectum is suspected, a stool sample is taken and examined for the presence of blood. Sometimes, there is such a small amount of blood that it can't be detected without a chemical test. In this case it is called occult — the Latin word for hidden — blood.

A barium X-ray is usually taken to determine the location of a suspected tumour. If a tumour is located, a colonoscope will be used to take a biopsy, and cells from it will be sent to a lab for examination.

Most intestinal problems do not turn out to be cancer. On the one hand, this is heartening, but many doctors worry that people who are embarrassed at the thought of an examination of the colon may use the information as an excuse to avoid checking into what might be an early cancer.

The treatment of colorectal cancer

Surgery, radiation therapy, or chemotherapy, and sometimes a combination of the three are used to treat colorectal cancer.

Surgery is most often chosen. Ressecting the colon may seem frightening, but the colon is not essential to life. If a section of the colon is removed, the two ends can be rejoined, and what remains will usually take over the organ's entire function.

If the rectum and the anus are cancerous, however, they must both be removed and a permanent colostomy performed. This means that the stools will be discharged into a plastic bag. While a procedure such as this is unpleasant to think about, many of us have met people with colostomies and just haven't realized it. Thousands of men and women with colostomies live perfectly normal lives.

The United Ostomy Association provides advice and emotional support to people, or the families of people, who have had colostomies. A local unit of the Canadian Cancer Society can put you in touch with such a group.

Although it is not used for cancer of the colon, radiation therapy is sometimes used for cancer of the rectum. Radiation therapy can also sometimes be used before surgery to shrink a tumour, or after surgery to mop up cancerous cells that may not have been accessible to the surgeon because of the shape of the tumour.

Chemotherapy is also sometimes used in the treatment of colorectal cancer, although few of the drugs that are currently available work well for either of these two types of carcinomas.

Cancer of the Uterus

What is the uterus?

The uterus, or womb, is a pear-shaped muscular organ in which the fetus develops during pregnancy. There are two parts to the uterus: the body and the cervix. The endometrium lines the organ's hollow body which tapers down into a narrower structure called the cervix, which leads into the vagina.

When a woman is not pregnant, the endometrium thickens monthly and is shed during menstruation.

There are two very different types of cancer of the uterus which is sometimes called uterine cancer: cancer of the cervix and cancer of the endometrium.

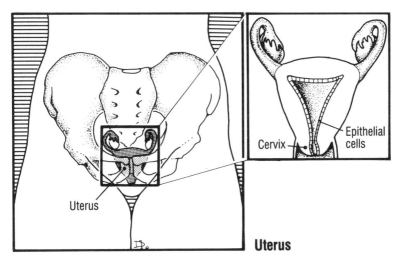

Uterus

Cancer of the Cervix

What is cancer of the cervix?

Cancer of the cervix develops in the epithelial cells that line the cervix and is sometimes called cervical cancer.

Most of the time, the cells of the cervix go through mild to severe changes, often over a period of years, before the cells actually change enough to be called cancer. These pre-cancerous changes are called dysplasia.

Who gets cancer of the cervix and what is the outlook?

Cancer of the cervix is diagnosed in approximately 1,500 Canadian women each year, mostly between the ages of 40 and 49. Cancer of the cervix used to be rare among women under the age of 40, but in recent years, more Canadian women in their 30s and even 20s have been developing this disease.

The cure rate for early cervical cancer is almost 100%. Most of the 600 Canadian women who die each year from this disease were diagnosed after it had already progressed to an advanced stage.

Surviving cervical cancer patients are considered cured five years after treatment has finished.

What causes cancer of the cervix and who is at high risk?

Although scientists do not know the exact cause of cervical cancer, they have been able to discover who has a higher-than-average risk of developing it. Women who begin their sex lives early, and women who have had many partners are more likely to get cervical cancer than other women.

There is some speculation as to why. The cells which line the cervical canal of a pre-adolescent female resemble columns and are called columnar cells. The cells that line the vagina, on the other hand, are shaped differently and are called squamous cells. These cells meet at the squamo-columnar junction and it is at this junction that most cancers of the cervix appear. During late adolescence, the columnar cells at the squamo-columnar junction are replaced by squamous cells. Researchers feel that while this change is taking place, women are more susceptible to genetic mutations. They also feel that the chance of a gene becoming mutated may increase when a woman has multiple sex partners who can introduce a virus or possibly other carcinogens to the area.

The signs and symptoms of cervical cancer

The first signs of cervical cancer are bleeding, often after sexual intercourse, or vaginal discharge. When cervical cancer is at a very early stage, however, there are usually no symptoms at all.

The diagnosis of cervical cancer

Cancer of the cervix can be diagnosed at an early stage by a simple, painless procedure called the Pap test which is described in detail on page 43.

The Pap test can detect dysplasia as well as early cancer. If there is any unusual bleeding or discharge from the cervix, or the results of a Pap test are positive, the doctor will perform a type of endoscopy. Using a colposcope, the doctor can examine the cervix for suspicious-looking tissue. If there is any, a biopsy will be taken and cells from it will be sent to a lab for microscopic examination.

The treatment of cervical cancer

If the biopsy indicates dysplasia, the doctor might decide to simply keep a close watch on the patient to see if these changes reverse themselves, which they sometimes do.

If the cells are severely dysplasic, or clearly cancerous, a conization is frequently performed. A cone-shaped sample of tissue about a centimeter thick is ressected surgically from the entire length of the cervix. Usually, it is only necessary to be in the hospital for a day or two when a conization is performed and there is only mild discomfort for a few days after that. A conization rarely effects a woman's sex life or her ability to have children.

Sometimes, when the doctor suspects that there are abnormal cells farther along the cervix than can be seen with a colposcope, a conization will be performed as a preventive measure. The cells that are removed when a conization is performed also provide a better sample for the biopsy than do cells from a Pap test or a colposcope biopsy.

Sometimes abnormal areas of the cervix are treated by cryosurgery which destroys tissue by freezing it. Other times, cancer cells are destroyed by heat. A new treatment is laser beam surgery. All three of these techniques can be done in the doctor's office with no general anaesthetic. They are only mildly uncomfortable and, like the conization, only rarely affect a woman's sex life or her ability to bear children.

On occasion, if a woman is not interested in having children and the doctor suspects that the disease may have spread, a hysterectomy will be performed. This is the surgical ressection of the entire cervix, the uterus, and sometimes the fallopian tubes as well.

When cancer of the cervix is more advanced, the treatment is more complicated.

Usually radiation therapy is chosen and occasionally, the doctor will combine radiation therapy with surgery.

When radiation therapy is chosen, both internal and external radiation are usually used. To radiate internally, radioactive pellets are inserted into the uterus for several days. Hospitalization is necessary during this time. External radiation can usually be performed without a hospital stay.

If radiotherapy is not successful, radical surgery is occasionally possible. On rare occasions, chemotherapy, which is considered experimental for cervical cancer, is used.

Endometrial Cancer

What is endometrial cancer?

Endometrial cancer develops in the endometrium, or lining of the body of the uterus.

The cells of the endometrium go through pre-cancerous changes called hyperplasia before they become abnormal enough to be called cancerous.

Who gets endometrial cancer and what is the outlook?

Endometrial cancer is diagnosed in approximately 2,300 Canadian women each year, mostly between the ages of 50 and 65. Approximately 500 Canadian women die from this type of cancer each year.

Early endometrial cancer can be successfully treated approximately 75% of the time. This rate could be as high as 90% if women recognized the symptoms of endometrial cancer and consulted a doctor immediately.

Five years after treatment is finished, surviving endometrial cancer patients are considered cured.

What causes endometrial cancer and who is at high risk?

Although the exact cause of endometrial cancer is unknown, studies have shown that certain women between the ages of 50 and 65 have a higher-than-average risk of developing this type of carcinoma. These are women who are overweight, diabetic, show signs of hypertension, have uterine bleeding after they have stopped menstruating, or continue to have periods after the age of 50. Women who have never borne children or take hormones, other than birth control pills, also have a higher-than-average risk of developing this disease.

Only half of the women who do develop endometrial cancer are in these high risk groups, however, and all women should be aware of the symptoms for endometrial cancer.

The signs and symptoms of endometrial cancer

The most common sign of endometrial cancer is unusual bleeding. For post menopausal women, this means any sort of bleeding; for women who are still menstruating, this means excessive bleeding during periods, or bleeding between periods.

The diagnosis of endometrial cancer

There are two types of tests for endometrial cancer. They are the Aspiration Curettage and the Dilation and Curettage of the uterus, usually referred to as a D and C.

The Aspiration Curettage is a simple procedure which can be performed in a doctor's office without a general anaesthetic. A thin tube is inserted through the cervix into the body of the uterus. Suction is used to take a biopsy which is sent to a lab for examination.

A general anaesthetic is necessary to do a D and C. The cervix is stretched, or dilated, and a tiny instrument is inserted into the uterine body. Cells from the lining of the body are then scraped off, or curettaged, and this biopsy is sent to a lab for examination.

The treatment of endometrial cancer

If very mild pre-cancerous changes are detected in the cells of the endometrium, the woman is usually watched carefully rather than treated; often these changes will reverse themselves. More serious cell changes often respond to hormone therapy. Drugs which bring on a menstrual period are given and the endometrium is shed along with the abnormal cells.

When cancerous cells are discovered, however, a hysterectomy is usually performed. The entire uterus, the fallopian tubes, and sometimes the lymph nodes nearby are surgically removed. In some cases, radiation therapy is added to the treatment. Sometimes internal radiation is chosen; other times external radiation is given.

If the doctor suspects that the cancer has metastasized to other parts of the body, chemotherapy will generally be added to the treatment.

Cancer of the Liver

What is the liver?

The liver is a complex organ which fills the upper right side of the abdomen and is protected by the rib cage.

The functions of the liver are too numerous to list completely, but they include: converting worn-out red blood cells to bile; producing proteins essential to blood clotting; and storing sugar and some vitamins.

What is cancer of the liver?

Most cancers of the liver are secondary tumours that have spread to the liver from other organs. Sometimes, however, primary liver cancer does develop in the epithelial cells of this organ.

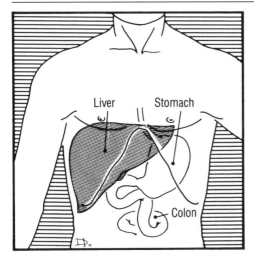

Liver

Who gets liver cancer and what is the outlook?

Liver cancer is diagnosed in approximately 400 Canadians each year. Because it is seldom detected at an early stage, this type of carcinoma can rarely be treated successfully, and almost everyone diagnosed with liver cancer will die of their disease.

What causes liver cancer and who is at high risk?

The exact cause of liver cancer is unknown, but studies have shown that exposure to certain chemicals, such as vinyl chloride, can increase a person's risk of developing this disease.

Athletes such as weight lifters who have taken large amounts of testosterone to increase their strength, also have a higher-than-average risk of developing liver cancer.

The signs and symptoms of liver cancer

There are no symptoms for liver cancer until the disease has progressed to an advanced stage. Even then, they are the same vague symptoms that others with cancers in organs deep in the abdomen complain of: mild discomfort, weakness, or loss of appetite.

The diagnosis of liver cancer

When liver cancer is suspected, X-rays are first taken to determine if there is a tumour. But to confirm the diagnosis, a biopsy must be performed. A local anaesthetic is first given and then a needle is inserted through the skin into the liver to obtain some tumour cells. These cells will be sent to a lab for microscopic examination.

If a diagnosis of liver cancer is confirmed, tests will be performed to determine if the cancer has spread.

The treatment of liver cancer

Radiation therapy or chemotherapy can sometimes extend the life of a patient with cancer of the liver. Most care for liver cancer is palliative, however, since it cannot be cured.

Cancer of the Bladder

What is the bladder?

The bladder is a muscular "balloon" that stores urine. The kidneys process the urine and from there it goes down a tube called the ureter to the bladder. From the bladder, the urine goes down another tube called the urethra and then leaves the body.

What is cancer of the bladder?

Bladder cancer develops in the epithelial cells of the bladder's inner lining. Most bladder cancer tumours are papillary

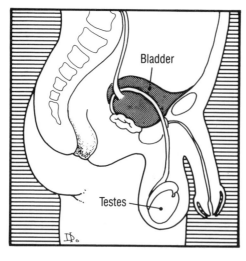

Bladder

tumours and look like tiny mushrooms whose stems are attached to the organ's lining. Some papillary tumours are benign rather than cancerous.

A less common type of bladder cancer called epidermoid carcinoma grows directly on the lining of the bladder and tends to invade the organ's muscular wall.

Who gets cancer of the bladder and what is the outlook?

Bladder cancer is diagnosed in approximately 3,200 Canadians each year. The majority are men over the age of 50; only one in three bladder cancer patients is a woman.

When it is diagnosed at an early stage, cancer of the bladder can be successfully treated. The approximately 1,000 Canadians whose bladder cancer was invasive by the time it was detected die each year.

Five years after treatment is discontinued, surviving bladder cancer patients are considered cured.

What causes bladder cancer and who is at high risk?

Although the exact cause of bladder cancer is unknown, certain people have a higher-than-average risk of developing this type of cancer. Studies have shown that exposure to certain industrial chemicals such as beta-napthylamine can increase a person's risk of bladder cancer. Other studies have linked tobacco, alcohol, and tea and coffee in large amounts over many years, to cancer of the bladder.

The signs and symptoms of bladder cancer

There is usually no pain associated with cancer of the bladder; the first sign is blood in the urine.

Blood in the urine is certainly not a sure sign of bladder cancer. If cancer of the bladder is suspected, a number of diagnostic tests must be done.

The diagnosis of bladder cancer

When a bladder tumour is suspected, the urine is analyzed to see if it contains any cancerous cells. The second test is a type of endoscopy. A cystoscope inserted into the bladder is used to locate and snip off a piece of the tumour. These cells are sent to a lab for microscopic examination. Sometimes, the entire tumour can be removed during the endoscopy procedure.

The treatment of bladder cancer

If the tumour cells are cancerous, radiation therapy or surgery will generally be used. Chemotherapy is sometimes used when the disease has metastasized to other parts of the body.

A single papillary tumour can often be removed with a cystoscope. Instead of biopsying a section of the tumour incisionally, the doctor will remove it entirely — called an excisional biopsy.

When there are several tumours, more extensive surgery is necessary. The tumours, as well as a margin of normal tissue, will be removed.

Radiation therapy is sometimes used as an alternative to surgery. With modern high voltage radiation equipment, X-rays can be directed at tumours in the bladder without permanent damage to other tissue. In Vancouver, at the B.C. Cancer Research Centre, experiments are also being conducted on bladder cancer patients using pion beams. The initial results look promising.

In a few cases, a cystectomy, a surgical procedure to remove the entire bladder, must be performed. In this case, a bag must be used to collect urine. The idea of living without a bladder sounds much worse than it really is. The United Ostomy Association which was formed to assist people without colons also provides information and emotional support to people who have had their bladders removed. Your local unit of the Canadian Cancer Society can put you in touch with a nearby branch.

Cancer of the Ovary

What are the ovaries?

The ovaries are the female reproductive organs in which the ova, or eggs, are formed. During the menstrual cycle, an egg is discharged from one of the ovaries and travels to the uterus by way of a fallopian tube. The ovaries also release the female hormone estrogen. When a woman gets to the age of about 48, the ovaries begin to produce less estrogen. At first, the menstrual periods become irregular and then stop completely. This is called menopause and women who have stopped menstruating are sometimes referred to as post menopausal women.

What is cancer of the ovaries?

Cancer of the ovaries, or ovarian cancer, develops in the epithelial cells that line the ovaries. Usually, only one of the two organs is affected.

Who gets cancer of the ovary and what is the outlook?

Ovarian cancer is diagnosed in approximately 1,500 Canadian women each year, mostly over the age of 50. Most of these women cannot be successfully treated unless the disease has been diagnosed at an early stage, which is rare. Each year, more than 1,000 Canadian women die of cancer of an ovary.

Five years after treatment, surviving ovarian cancer patients are considered cured.

What causes cancer of the ovary and who is at high risk?

While the exact cause of ovarian cancer is unknown, some studies have shown that women who have had a close relative

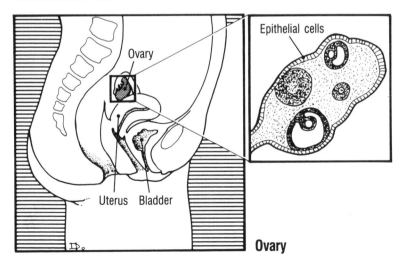

Ovary

with ovarian cancer have a higher-than-average risk of developing this disease. Other studies show that women who are infertile are also at a higher-than-average risk. Studies to relate ovarian cancer to dietary habits are also being conducted.

The signs and symptoms of cancer of the ovary

Because the ovaries are located deep within the pelvis, there are rarely any symptoms — no pain, no bleeding, and no obvious swelling — until the disease has progressed to an advanced stage. When it is discovered at an early stage, it is usually by chance during an examination for some unrelated problem.

The diagnosis of cancer of the ovary

If cancer of the ovaries is suspected, a number of diagnostic tests are performed. X-rays and ultrasound are used to determine the size and location of a suspected tumour.

If a tumour is located, a minor surgical procedure called laparoscopy will be performed. This involves cutting a tiny "peep hole" in the abdomen so a biopsy of the ovary can be taken. Cells from the biopsy are sent to a lab for microscopic examination.

The treatment of cancer of the ovary

If an ovarian tumour is cancerous, a surgical procedure called a oophorectomy will be performed. Both ovaries, the fallopian tubes, and the uterus are generally removed whether or not it is suspected that the tumour has metastasized.

If it is obvious that the cancer has spread, radiation therapy, or chemotherapy, and sometimes both, can be used.

Cancer of the Pancreas

What is the pancreas?

The pancreas is a gland that is located behind the stomach. It produces proteins which help digest food and insulin that regulates the amount of sugar in the blood.

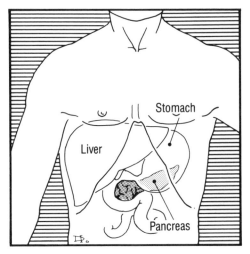

Pancreas

What is cancer of the pancreas?

Most cancers of the pancreas develop in the cells that make up the organ's duct system. Occasionally, however, cancer of the pancreas begins in the cells that produce insulin, the Islets of Langerhans.

Who gets cancer of the pancreas and what is the outlook?

Every year, nearly 2,000 Canadians develop cancer of the pancreas. Few patients with this type of carcinoma survive.

What causes cancer of the pancreas and who is at high risk?

Some studies have linked cancer of the pancreas with cigarette smoking, although scientists do not understand why.

The signs and symptoms of cancer of the pancreas

Cancer of the pancreas is rarely discovered at an early stage. There are no symptoms — no pain or swelling — until it has advanced, and by that time, a patient will usually only notice a vague pain in the abdomen or back. Sometimes, there is weight loss, nausea, or a feeling of general weakness.

The diagnosis of cancer of the pancreas

When cancer of the pancreas is suspected, a barium X-ray is taken; when barium is swallowed prior to an X-ray, a much clearer picture of the organ can be obtained.

Recently, doctors in some hospitals have been using CT scans or ultrasound to locate tumours in the pancreas and determine their size.

When it has been established that there is a tumour, a biopsy will be taken to determine if its cells are cancerous. To biopsy the pancreas, a surgical procedure called a laparotomy is almost always performed, although in some hospitals a minor surgical technique using a needle to suction cells is sometimes used.

The treatment of cancer of the pancreas

If a tumour in a pancreas is cancerous, it can sometimes be entirely removed by surgery. Most of the time, however, it is only possible to remove part of it.

Radiation or chemotherapy are often given after surgery, and while these two types of treatment usually decrease discomfort, they do not usually prolong life for very long. If there is pain, certain nerves leading to the pancreas can sometimes be blocked.

Cancer of the Kidney

What are the kidneys?

The kidneys are a pair of organs located behind the liver and stomach near the spine, one on either side. The kidneys help remove wastes from our bodies by making urine. They do this by filtering urea, salt and other substances from the blood as it flows through them. Three tubes enter each kidney at the point where the organ indents: the renal vein; the renal artery; and the ureter, which is the long tube down which urine flows to the bladder. The shell enclosing the kidney is called the capsule. Inside the kidney, blood is filtered by thousands of

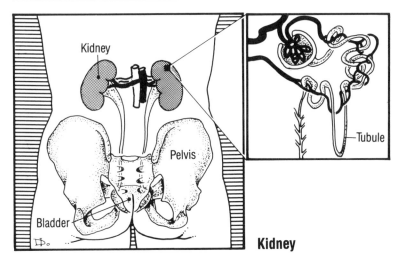

Kidney

filament-like tubes called renal tubules. The renal pelvis collects the urine that is produced, and funnels it into the ureter.

The kidneys also manufacture and secrete a variety of hormones.

There are two very different types of kidney cancer. One occurs in adults; the other almost always occurs in children and is called Wilm's tumour. Wilm's tumour is one of the only carcinomas that affects children.

Adult Cancer of the Kidney

What is cancer of the kidney in adults?

Most of the time, cancer of the kidney in adults develops in the cells that form the lining of a renal tubule. In rare cases, a tumour will begin to grow on the renal capsule itself.

Who gets adult kidney cancer and what is the outlook?

Kidney cancer is diagnosed in approximately 1,000 Canadian adults each year, most of whom are over the age of 40. Twice as many males develop kidney cancer as females. About a third of the adults who develop this disease can be successfully treated; approximately 600 adult Canadians die of kidney cancer each year.

Five years after treatment is finished, surviving adult kidney cancer patients are considered cured.

What causes adult kidney cancer and who is at high risk?

The causes of adult kidney cancer are unknown, but certain people are considered to have a higher-than-average risk of developing this disease. Some studies show that people who smoke have a higher-than-average risk of developing kidney cancer and studies which may link certain dietary habits to kidney cancer are now being conducted.

The signs and symptoms of adult kidney cancer

Kidney cancer in adults is sometimes suspected because of blood in the urine, although this can also be the sign of many urinary disorders other than cancer.

Other times, patients feel a lump in the abdomen and vague pain. Some people with kidney cancer complain of weight loss, or fatigue, but because these symptoms are common to so many other medical problems, the disease often remains undetected until it has reached an advanced stage.

The diagnosis of adult kidney cancer

When cancer of the kidney is suspected, dye to highlight the kidneys is injected into the bloodstream and then an X-ray is taken. CT scans and ultrasound are also sometimes used to get a better idea of the size of the tumour and its exact location.

If the doctor suspects that the cancer has metastasized, bone scans or chest X-rays will be taken in an attempt to pinpoint the metastases. Most often, kidney cancer in adults will spread to the lungs and bones first.

The treatment of adult kidney cancer

When a cancerous kidney tumour is still localized and the second kidney is working well, the cancerous kidney, a section of normal tissue, and the lymph nodes nearby will most likely be removed. This type of operation is called a nephrectomy. Because a remaining kidney will take over the function that was performed by the two organs, a person can lead a normal life with one kidney.

Sometimes, radiation therapy is used before this type of surgery to shrink the tumour. Other times, it is used after surgery to mop up any cancerous cells that were not able to be surgically removed.

Radiation therapy is generally used when kidney cancer has metastasized. When it has spread to the bones, radiation will often relieve the pain caused by the secondary tumour. In some cases, chemotherapy is given, but anti-cancer drugs for this type of cancer are still considered experimental.

Kidney Cancer in Children — Wilm's Tumour

What is Wilm's tumour?

Wilm's tumour, which is sometimes referred to as nephroblastoma, develops in the epithelial cells that line the kidney. This type of carcinoma rarely affects both kidneys.

Who gets Wilm's tumour and what is the outlook?

Approximately 270 Canadian children, mostly between the ages of one and eight, are diagnosed with Wilm's tumour each year. Due to recent advances in chemotherapy, 80% of them can be treated successfully.

What causes Wilm's tumour and who is at high risk?

The exact causes of Wilm's tumour are unknown, but certain children have a higher-than-average risk of developing this disease.

If one child in a family has had Wilm's tumour, a second child will have a higher-than-average risk of developing the disease and will be monitored carefully. Children whose eyes lack an iris (the coloured portion of the eye), also have a higher-than-average risk of developing Wilm's tumour, as do children with other developmental abnormalities.

The signs and symptoms of Wilm's tumour

The most common symptom of Wilm's tumour is a lump in the belly, or a swollen abdomen. Approximately 25% of Wilm's tumour patients produce blood in the urine, but often the amount is so small that it can only be detected by a chemical test. The complaints of many children are vague: low fever, fatigue, loss of appetite, weight loss, and anemia.

The diagnosis of Wilm's tumour

The diagnosis for Wilm's tumour is the same as for adult cancer of the kidney.

The treatment of Wilm's tumour

Surgery, radiation therapy, and chemotherapy, and sometimes a combination of all three are used in the treatment of Wilm's tumour.

When a kidney is removed by surgery, the operation is called a nephrectomy. Usually, Wilm's tumour affects only one kidney and a child can lead a normal life if a kidney is removed. When it affects both kidneys, one tumour is usually very small. In these rare situations, one kidney and the small tumour on the second kidney can generally be removed without removing the entire second organ.

Radiation therapy is often used after surgery to guard against recurrence. Sometimes, if a tumour is very large, it will be shrunk by radiation therapy before surgery. Radiation therapy is not used on children under the age of two.

Chemotherapy is also used in almost all cases of Wilm's tumour, and this type of treatment accounts for the fact that eight out of 10 children with Wilm's tumour can be successfully treated.

The Lymphomas

Lymphomas are cancers of the lymphocytes, the white blood cells of the lymphatic system.

Hodgkin's disease and non-Hodgkin's lymphoma

What is the lymphatic system?

The lymphatic system is made up of several parts. A network of vessels — similar to blood vessels — transports the colourless lymphatic fluid, called lymph, around the body; lymph bathes all of the body's cells to prevent them from drying out. At different points along the route are lymph nodes which act as filters, sifting out any impurities, like bacteria for example, that the lymph picks up. These nodes are made up of clusters of infection-fighting white blood cells called T and B lymphocytes.

What is cancer of the lymphatic system?

Lymphoma is the general term for cancers that develop in the tissue of the lymphatic system. It is the lymphocyte cells that form the lymph nodes which become cancerous.

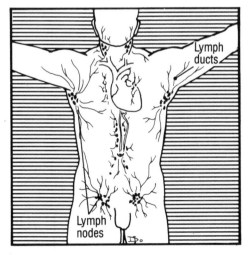

The Lymphatic System

There are basically two types of lymphomas. One is Hodgkin's disease. The other is non-Hodgkin's lymphoma. Both are cancers of the lymphatic system, but they differ in several ways.

In Hodgkin's disease, particular cells called Reed-Sternberg cells can always be found when the patient's lymph nodes are examined microscopically. With non-Hodgkin's lymphoma, there are no Reed-Sternberg cells.

As lymphomas progress, more and more cancerous lymphocyte cells are produced, leaving fewer and fewer normal cells to fight infection. For this reason, lymphoma patients often develop various types of infections.

Who gets cancer of the lymphatic system and what is the outlook?

Hodgkin's disease is diagnosed in about 1,000 Canadians each year. About 1,800 people develop non-Hodgkin's lymphoma.

The majority of Hodgkin's disease patients are between the ages of 20 and 40, although this type of cancer sometimes develops in people as young as 10 and as old as 70.

The majority of people with non-Hodgkin's lymphoma are between the ages of 55 and 70, although children sometimes develop this disease.

Approximately 80% of Hodgkin's disease patients can be successfully treated. As few as 20 years ago, only 20% of these patients could be cured. Today, approximately 200 Canadians die each year of this type of lymphoma.

The success rate for the treatment of non-Hodgkin's lymphoma is not as high. Approximately 1,200 Canadians die each year from non-Hodgkin's lymphoma.

When they have been off treatment for eight years, surviving lymphoma patients are considered cured.

What causes lymphoma and who is at high risk?

Although the exact cause of lymphoma is unknown, a growing number of researchers believe that people who develop this type of cancer have some sort of defect in their immune system which makes them less able to fight off a certain type of virus if they are exposed to it.

Lymphomas are less common among people who have grown up in underdeveloped countries where they have been exposed to diseases during childhood. When people are exposed to disease and survive it, they often become immune to that disease, meaning that their bodies have produced antibodies that protect them from developing the disease again. For this reason, people get chicken pox only once.

The signs and symptoms of lymphoma

The first sign of a lymphoma is usually a painless, swollen lymph node in the neck, armpit, or groin; a painful, inflamed node is usually a symptom of something other than cancer.

Occasionally, there is swelling, fever, sweating, shortness of breath, back pain, unexplained weight loss, unexplained itchiness, or nausea. But since these are also the symptoms of dozens of other medical problems, lymphomas can remain undetected for some time.

The diagnosis of lymphoma

If there is something suspicious about a lymph node, it will be surgically removed and studied in a lab. If the cells are cancerous, tests to determine the extent of the cancer will be performed.

Chest X-rays are taken to see if the lymphoma has spread into the chest area. Blood tests are taken, and a lymphangiography is also performed. During a lymphangiography, a type of dye that is impervious to X-rays is injected into the lymphatic system. When the X-ray is taken, the lymphatic system is outlined and the doctor can see the extent to which the disease has spread.

If it is suspected that a lymphoma has spread to other parts of the body, a CT scan, a bone marrow test, and biopsies of suspected organs will be taken.

The treatment of lymphoma

Because lymphomas are systemic diseases — diseases that spread throughout a system — surgery is rarely used. Radiation therapy, chemotherapy, and sometimes a combination of the two are more often used.

Radiation therapy is usually the treatment for a lymphoma that has not widely spread.

Chemotherapy alone or in combination with radiotherapy is chosen when it has been determined that the disease has spread.

The Myelomas

Myelomas are cancers of particular white blood cells called plasma cells. Plasma cells start off as B lymphocytes and then move into the lymphatic system where they mature further into plasma cells. Plasma cells are stored in bone marrow.

Multiple Myeloma

What is multiple myeloma?

Multiple myeloma, like lymphoma, is a cancer of the white blood cells. Lymphomas, however, are cancers of the lymphocytes while multiple myelomas involve plasma cells which develop from B lymphocytes and then move to the bone marrow where they are stored.

When a person develops myeloma, too many plasma cells are produced. What's worse, these plasma cells are not mature. They are unable to perform their job of producing antibodies to fight infection. They do produce antibodies — too many in fact — but they are abnormal. They pour into the bloodstream and lymphatic system where they interfere with the body's normal functions.

Multiple myeloma patients also sometimes develop diseases such as pneumonia or kidney infections because they have lost the ability to produce the antibodies that can fight infection.

Who gets multiple myeloma and what is the outlook?

Every year, approximately 600 Canadians, mostly over the age of 50, develop multiple myeloma. Due to recent developments in chemotherapy, remissions can be achieved for many multiple myeloma patients. Unfortunately, these remissions rarely last for more than a few years.

What causes multiple myeloma and who is at high risk?

The causes of multiple myeloma are unknown although a few studies have shown that people who have been exposed to excessive amounts of radiation have a higher-than-average risk of developing this disease.

The signs and symptoms of multiple myeloma

Multiple myeloma is usually discovered when a person has pain in the bones. This is caused by the abnormal number of plasma cells in the bone marrow. Sometimes, multiple myeloma patients complain of fatigue because the abnormal plasma cells are interfering with the production of red blood cells that carry oxygen to the body. Some people suffer from nose bleeds, bleeding gums, or bruising because fewer platelets, which control bleeding, are produced.

The diagnosis of multiple myeloma

When multiple myeloma is suspected, X-rays are taken to locate the tumour.

Since cancerous plasma cells produce abnormal proteins which are eventually excreted in the urine, multiple myeloma is one of the few cancers that can sometimes be diagnosed through a urine sample.

The conclusive test for multiple myeloma, however, is a bone marrow aspiration and usually a bone biopsy as well.

For the bone marrow aspiration, an area on either the breast bone or the pelvis is anaesthetized and a thin needle is inserted into the marrow of the bone. A small bit of tissue is then suctioned out and cells from it are sent to a lab for microscopic examination. The aspiration procedure is usually painful, but only for a brief moment.

The treatment of multiple myeloma

Chemotherapy is most often used to treat multiple myeloma. Sometimes, radiation therapy is also used because it can shrink collections of cancerous cells, enabling the body to repair the bone damage that myeloma can cause. Radiation therapy can also relieve pain caused by multiple myeloma.

When a multiple myeloma patient is in remission, bone marrow aspirations, blood tests, and urine samples are still taken frequently to ensure that the patient does not go out of remission undetected.

The Leukemias

What is leukemia?

The word leukemia literally means white blood. Leukemias are cancers of various types of leukocytes, or white blood cells, that are produced in the bone marrow.

If you've read the sections on lymphomas and multiple myelomas, you're probably a bit confused.

When a person develops lymphoma, specific white blood cells of the lymphatic system, called T and B lymphocytes, become cancerous.

When a person develops multiple myeloma, white blood cells called plasma cells, which are stored in bone marrow, become cancerous. Plasma cells actually develop from B lymphocytes.

The bone marrow itself also produces blood cells. Red blood cells, for example, normally deliver oxygen to body tissues; white blood cells called granulocytes (or polys) fight infection in the bloodstream; and platelets control and prevent bleeding.

When a person develops leukemia, too many abnormal white blood cells are produced. Eventually, these immature white blood cells monopolize the bone marrow which then produces too few red blood cells, and insufficient platelets.

Who gets leukemia and what is the outlook?

Leukemia is usually thought of as a childhood disease because of the publicity surrounding childhood leukemia which is one of the great success stories of cancer treatment. More adults than children, however, are affected by leukemia.

Each year, one of the various types of leukemia is diagnosed in approximately 1,900 Canadian adults. Acute myelogenous leukemia, usually called AML, is the most common type of adult leukemia. Leukemia is more difficult to successfully treat in adults than in children; about 1,400 adults die of this type of cancer every year.

Approximately 280 Canadian children are diagnosed with leukemia each year, the majority of whom develop acute lymphoblastic leukemia, or ALL. More than half of these children can be treated successfully.

The overall cure rate for all people with all types of leukemia, however, is only about 20%. Although leukemia patients must survive for five years after treatment to be considered cured, it is ususual for a patient to go out of remission two years after treatment is finished.

What causes leukemia and who is at high risk?

The exact causes of leukemia are unknown, but researchers have been able to show that certain people have a higher-than-average risk of developing this kind of cancer.

Excessive exposure to radiation or certain drugs increases a person's risk of developing leukemia. Some patients who are treated for other kinds of cancer such as Hodgkin's disease, cancer of the ovary, or multiple myeloma, develop leukemia a number of years later.

The signs and symptoms of leukemia

Sometimes, leukemia is detected when the bone marrow's over-production of abnormal white blood cells interferes with the production of red blood cells. When there are too few red blood cells, too little oxygen will be delivered to the body's cells, and the patient will complain of fatigue.

Other times, leukemia is discovered because too few platelets are being produced. In this case, the signs will be bruising, frequent nose bleeds, or bleeding of the gums.

In still other cases, leukemia is suspected because the leukemic white blood cells are not able to fight infection and something as minor as a sore throat does not improve.

The diagnosis of leukemia

When there are suspicious symptoms, two diagnostic tests are usually performed.

One is a simple test where blood is taken from a vein in the finger or arm and tested to reveal the presence of cancerous blood cells.

The other test is a bone marrow aspiration. First, a local anaesthetic is injected into the hip, and then a thin needle is inserted into the marrow of a bone. A tiny amount of bone marrow is removed by suction and cells from it are sent to the lab for examination. A bone marrow aspiration is usually painful, but only for a brief moment.

The treatment of leukemia

The objective of the treatment for leukemia is to destroy the cancerous white blood cells and increase the production of the normal types of blood cells.

Chemotherapy in two phases is used to treat leukemia. The first phase generally lasts for several months and causes more adverse side-effects than the second phase which is called maintenance therapy and generally lasts for about two years. (See page 77.)

Sometimes a single drug is used during the first phase of treatment, but more often a combination of cancer-killing chemicals are administered to the patient over a period of months. Doctors have achieved remissions in a high percentage of patients with leukemia. When a patient is in remission, all, or at least part of, the signs of the disease will disappear.

During maintenance therapy, most patients can live a fairly normal life except, perhaps, for the few days a month when strong anti-cancer drugs are given.

Most adults with acute leukemia do not remain in remission for more than a few months or years. Many children, on the other hand, have been in remission for as long as 15 years and are considered cured.

Chemotherapy kills almost all of the bone marrow cells. Because bone marrow cells reproduce very quickly, they soon increase to the normal number. If the treatment is successful, the new bone marrow cells will be normal instead of leukemic.

After the first phase of chemotherapy is finished, radiation therapy is also sometimes used to treat certain types of leukemia. The purpose of radiation therapy is to kill any leukemic cells that have spread to the brain. Many anti-cancer chemicals do not reach the brain because of what is called the blood-brain barrier which prevents chemicals from moving into the brain from the bloodstream. Radiation to the brain, however, will often mop up the cancer cells that have been missed by chemotherapy.

An experimental type of treatment for acute leukemia is beginning to yield some initially promising results. It is called bone marrow transplantation and it seems to work best on patients who are under the age of 40.

A bone marrow transplantation can only be used when there is a suitable person to donate bone marrow to the leukemia patient. It must be someone, usually a brother or sister, whose cells have the same HLA markers (see page 20) as the leukemia patient's cells. If these markers are different, the patient will perceive the donated marrow as alien and reject it.

Prior to a bone marrow transplantation, all the bone marrow cells of the leukemia patient are destroyed by very strong chemicals. Then, about 500 mL of bone marrow is removed by suction from the hip bone of the donor who is under general anaesthetic. It is not a painful procedure, but usually the donor's hip area will be sore for a few days. In fact, bone marrow is extracted from the donor by the same procedure that is used to aspirate bone marrow from a leukemia patient for testing, except that more marrow is required for a transplant than for a test.

The marrow is then administered to the leukemia patient in basically the same way as a blood transfusion. The hope is that the patient's body will accept the donor's bone marrow and begin producing normal blood cells.

Patients in remission are usually put on maintenance drug therapy, sometimes for several years, in the hope of ensuring that leukemic cells do not reappear.

The Sarcomas

Sarcomas are cancers of mesodermal cells: bone, muscle, cartilage, tendon, and ligament cells which form supportive and connective tissues. Bone tissue is most often involved in these types of cancer.

Osteogenic Sarcoma

What is osteogenic sarcoma?

Osteogenic sarcoma is the most common form of the sarcomas, which are very rare. Osteogenic sarcoma develops in bone itself, rather than in bone marrow which is where leukemia and multiple myeloma develop.

Most bone cancers have spread from another organ and are therefore secondary, rather than primary, cancers. There are, however, a number of different types of primary bone cancer, the most common of which is osteogenic sarcoma. This type of bone cancer can develop in long bones, flat bones, the pelvis, or the spine. Long bones, however, are the most common site for this uncommon disease. Terry Fox died of osteogenic sarcoma of the leg. On the other hand, United States Senator Edward Kennedy's son, Edward Kennedy Jr., was cured of this disease.

Who gets bone cancer and what is the outlook?

Fewer than 100 Canadians develop osteogenic sarcoma each year; most who do are under the age of 20. Only a few years ago, this type of cancer was fatal for eight out of 10 patients. Today, however, because of advances in chemotherapy, approximately 60% of osteogenic sarcoma patients can be successfully treated. Because it spreads very quickly through the bloodstream, osteogenic sarcomas must be diagnosed at an early stage for treatment to be successful.

Five years after treatment, surviving osteogenic sarcoma patients are considered cured.

What causes osteogenic sarcoma and who is at high risk?

The causes and risk factors for this type of cancer are unknown.

The signs and symptoms of osteogenic sarcoma

The first sign of this type of cancer is usually pain in the bone where the tumour is located, followed by swelling.

The diagnosis of osteogenic sarcoma

Bone scans can determine the location of osteogenic sarcoma, but in order to confirm that the tumour cells are cancerous, a biopsy must be performed. A fragment of the tumour is surgically removed and sent to the lab for microscopic examination.

The treatment of osteogenic sarcoma

Surgery, or radiation therapy, followed by chemotherapy are usually used to treat osteogenic sarcoma. Usually the affected limb is amputated, although recently, some research centres have been experimenting with radiation therapy so that the affected limb can be saved.

After surgery, chemotherapy is given to kill any cancer cells that may have already metastasized. Because of recent advances in anti-cancer drugs, 60% of patients with osteogenic sarcoma are now able to be successfully treated.

Cancer of the Brain

What is brain cancer?

Primary cancers do begin in the brain, but it is far more common for cancer to metastasize to the brain from other organs. On the other hand, cancers that develop in the tissues of the brain rarely spread to other parts of the body.

Who gets brain cancer and what is the outlook?

About 1,300 Canadians develop primary brain cancer every year. Two hundred of these people are children. Few brain cancer patients can be successfully treated, and approximately 1,100 primary brain cancer patients die each year.

What causes brain cancer and who is at high risk?

The causes and risk factors for this type of cancer are unknown.

The signs and symptoms of brain cancer

A person is usually alerted to brain cancer because of headache; as the tumour grows and presses against normal brain tissue, it causes pain. There are times, however, when a person with a brain tumour becomes nauseated, dizzy, or loses the sense of taste or smell. About a third of brain cancer patients have convulsions, the correct term for what are sometimes called seizures.

The diagnosis of brain cancer

When a brain tumour is suspected, the retina of the eye and the optic nerve are examined. X-rays are also taken. The CT scanner has made the diagnosis of brain tumours much simpler and is used whenever possible.

The treatment of brain cancer

The treatment for cancer of the brain is surgery, radiation therapy and sometimes a combination of the two. Because of the blood-brain barrier, few chemicals injected into the bloodstream reach the brain and for this reason, chemotherapy is not frequently used to treat brain cancer.

A brain tumour, or as much of it as possible, will be surgically ressected if it is accessible, whether it is cancerous or benign. Brain tumours are always dangerous since there is no room for expansion inside the skull. A tumour presses against normal brain tissue and causes damage.

Radiation therapy is often used when a brain tumour cannot be entirely removed by surgery.

When chemotherapy is used, it is sometimes injected directly into the brain through a small, implanted tube. A relatively new group of anti-cancer drugs called nitrosoureas have been effective in some cases.

Bibliography

American Cancer Society, *Unproven Methods of Cancer Management*. New York: American Cancer Society, 1971.

Adams, D., & Deveau, E. *Coping with Childhood Cancer*. Reston, Virginia: Reston Publishing Co., 1984.

Brody, J., with Holleb, A. *You Can Fight Cancer and Win*. New York: McGraw-Hill, 1978.

Cameron, E., & Pauling, L. *Cancer and Vitamin C*. New York: Warner Books, 1981.

Furman, E. *A Child's Parent Dies*. New Haven: Yale University Press, 1974.

Glucksberg, H., & Singer, J. *Cancer Care*. New York: Scribner's, 1982.

Gonick, L., & Wheelis, M. *The Cartoon Guide to Genetics*. New York: Barnes and Noble Books, 1983.

Harsanyi, Z. & Hutton, R. *Genetic Prophecy: Beyond the Double Helix*. New York: Rawson Wade, 1981.

Jackson, E. *Telling a Child About Death*. New York: Hawthorne, 1965.

Koocher, G. & O'Malley, J. *The Damocles Syndrome*. New York: McGraw-Hill, 1981.

Kubler-Ross, E. *On Death and Dying*. New York: Macmillan, 1969.

Kubler-Ross, E. *Questions and Answers on Death and Dying*. New York: Macmillan, 1974.

Kuber-Ross, E. *To Live Until We Say Goodbye*. New York: Prentice-Hall, 1975.

Levitt, P. & Guralnick, E. *The Cancer Reference Book*. New York: Facts on File Inc., 1979.

MacDonald, J. *When Cancer Strikes*. Toronto: McClelland and Stewart, 1979.

Morra, M. & Potts, E. *Choices: Realistic Alternatives in Cancer Treatment*. New York: Avon, 1980.

Pendleton, E. *Too Old to Cry. . . Too Young to Die*. Nashville: Thomas Nelson, 1980.

Prescott, D. & Flexer, A. *Cancer: The Misguided Cell*. New York: Scribner's, 1982.

Rosenbaum, E. *Living With Cancer*. New York: Praeger, 1975.

Schiff, H. *The Bereaved Parent*. New York: Penguin, 1978.

Sontag, S. *Illness as Metaphor*. New York: Farrar, Straus & Giroux, 1978.

Terry, L. & Horn, D. *To Smoke or Not to Smoke*. New York: Lothrop, Lee and Shepard Co., 1969.

Thomas, L. *The Lives of a Cell: Notes of a Biology Watcher.* New York: Bantam, 1975.

Whelan, E. *Preventing Cancer.* New York: W.W. Norton, 1978.

Wolfe, A. *Helping Your Child to Understand Death.* New York: Child Study Association of America, 1958.

Index